What Makes the Crops Rejoice

What Makes the Crops Rejoice =

An Introduction to Gardening

ROBERT HOWARD
with ERIC SKJEI

Illustrations by Barbara Bash

LITTLE, BROWN AND COMPANY
Boston Toronto

FIRST EDITION

Library of Congress Cataloging-in-Publication Data

Howard, Robert, 1946–
What makes the crops rejoice.

Bibliography: p.
1. Gardening.   I. Skjei, Eric W.   II. Title.
SB453.H784   1986   635   85-20983
ISBN 0-316-37474-1

RRD VA

Designed by Patricia Girvin Dunbar

*Published simultaneously in Canada
by Little, Brown & Company (Canada) Limited*

PRINTED IN THE UNITED STATES OF AMERICA

For Ethan, Paolo, and Sam
— R.H.

For Janive and the memory of R.O.
— E.S.

What makes the crops rejoice, beneath what star
To plough, and when to wed the vines to elms,
The care of cattle, how to rear a flock,
How much experience thrifty bees require,
Of these, Maecenas, I begin to sing.
— Virgil, *Georgics,*
Book I, 1–5

Contents

Acknowledgments

Our heartfelt gratitude to the many people who gave us a hand.

Solange Gignac and her staff at the Helen Fowler Library, Denver Botanic Gardens, facilitated our research over a number of years.

Barbara Kaufman took a walk in Central Park for us, as well as sending us material on Olmsted. William Alex, of the Frederick Law Olmsted Association, and Shary Page Berg, of the Frederick Law Olmsted National Historic Site, were generous with their assistance. At Stanford University, Roxanne Nilan, Archives Librarian, and Gerard Koskovich, who kindly made his own research available, helped our understanding of Olmsted's role in shaping that campus.

The chapter about Alan Chadwick could not have been written without the friendly guidance of many of Alan's colleagues, students, and companions. Thank you, Virginia Baker, Betsy Bruneau, Louise Cain, Seddon Chadwick, Father Michael Culligan, Steve Decater, Acacia Downs, Eva Fosselius, John and Robin Jeavons, Steve Kaffka, Paul and Charlene Lee, Fred Marshall, Dean McHenry, Jim and Beth Nelson, Wendy Johnson Rudnick, Page Smith, Chris and

Stephanie Tebbut, Freya von Moltke, Bernard Taper, Richard Wilson, and Michael Zander.

And to those who helped us put the manuscript in presentable shape, Linda Sutton Arnoldi and Diana Gray, our warm appreciation.

We thank Johns Hopkins University Press for permission to quote from *The Papers of Frederick Law Olmsted* the planting directions that appear on pages 62–64; Father Michael Culligan for the Chadwick letter that appears on pages 119–120 and for the remarks that appear on page 123; and Freya von Moltke for permission to use the quotations that appear on pages 106 and 108.

We appreciate the help given us by Mr. Richard Wilson for permission to reprint the Covelo Garden Project logbook entry that appears on page 117, and the British Architectural Library, R.I.B.A. Mss Coll. (the Misses J., S., and J. C. Ridley) for the Lutyens cartoon on page 71. Several of Barbara Bash's original drawings are modeled on earlier art or photographs, and we wish to acknowledge the following for allowing us to draw from the earlier sources: illustration on page 40, Newsweek Book Division; on page 61, University of Massachusetts Press, and courtesy National Park Service, Frederick Law Olmsted National Historic Site; on page 71, A & C Black Ltd., publisher of Sutton Palmer's *Surrey*; on page 83, Jane Brown; on page 87, National Portrait Library; and on page 112, Virginia Baker, Alan Chadwick Society.

PART ONE

Nature's Garden

Through the Garden Gate

I first met Alan Chadwick in the summer of 1971, at the Garden Project he directed at the University of California, Santa Cruz. The Civil Rights Movement, Vietnam, the counterculture — all these had given rise to a radical young weed. I was disenchanted, longing to find my place in the world.

On a July morning I walked into the garden, pack on my back, and started work that same day, digging beds. My spade slipped into the deep rich soil. I added compost, with its earthy odor of life and death. The smells, the soil, the peace one feels working outdoors, using well-crafted hand tools, all made me feel like a countryman.

On that summer day, the garden was in its glory. Alan and his apprentices had been making it thrive for four years already. It was a whole world, lush with flowers, seeds, leaves, compost, chickens, cycles, and routines, turning out lettuce, peas, beans, and gardeners. Red flowers of scarlet runner beans fluttered on the vine like butterflies. Long beds of Bibb lettuce betokened a cornucopia of fresh salads. Gerry Hoek and Glory of Heemstede dahlias waited to grace banquet tables. Looking at the garden, I found it hard

3

Garden gate, Santa Cruz Garden Project

to believe that it had been started on an impoverished hillside of poison oak and blackberry brambles when Alan first arrived. When I met him, it was easy to believe.

For me, Alan personified the garden world. He was energetic and hardworking, knowledgeable and highly trained. But for all that, his way of gardening went beyond simple professionalism. He embodied instead a Renaissance attitude about it, one that drew as much from poetry, history, theater, and folklore as from botany and horticulture. One that taught that the cultivation of nature is a high calling, one in which human beings can find strength beyond sustenance. Alan's garden is a sacred ground, where men and nature meet.

Digging was not the only thing a new apprentice did, I soon found out. I also poured kitchen wastes on the compost pile, sowed pea seed, cut dahlias, harvested lettuce, and learned another new chore every day.

My day began with feeding the chickens. Before sunrise I

4

got up and entered the garden through the north gate. On my right was the greenhouse, with its year-round, steamy-windowpane promise of new life. Inside, seedlings radiated the green glow of spring. Nearby, cold frames harbored young plants in transition to outdoor beds. On my left, the subtle smell of lilies wafted up to greet me.

To the chalet to warm up the mash I went, then to the coop. The minute I walked in the gate, a young rooster always charged me. I always booted him out of the way; he always came flying right back. He never learned; neither did I.

Next I went to the kitchen and picked up the bucketful of kitchen scraps, juices, and sour milk that was collected there. Bubbling and simmering with microbiotic life, it smelled like sour beer. But as soon as it hit the compost pile, that smell vanished, absorbed on contact.

The garden was situated on a peninsula that stretches its arm around Monterey Bay; it looked back east across an expanse of water to the sunrise. Many mornings the sun would come up out of a low-lying fog bank that covered the bay: the air would gradually lighten, then up it would pop like a big orange jack-in-the-box.

In the cool of the morning, when the juices were still full and fresh in the lettuce and cabbage, and the fragrance still alive in the flower, was the time to harvest. This was the time to water too, so that a reservoir of soil moisture would be available to support transpiration through the day. Later, in the heat of the afternoon, leaves turn away from the sun, wilting in a natural self-protective measure to conserve moisture.

When the harvesting and watering were done, it was time for breakfast on the deck of the chalet, and for Alan's mid-morning talk. The large deck was planted on three sides with climbing roses, the old-fashioned kinds, redolent of old-world perfumes and rural graciousness, of leaded windows giving out onto estate gardens with carefully tended lawns and primulas wending their way down to the wood.

Into the center of this garden stage would stride a tall, white-haired Englishman, an ex–Shakespearean actor and naval officer whose voice could whisper with enchantment or crackle with command, whose dark eyes could glow with charm or blaze with fury. Sixty-two years old at the time, deeply tanned, trim and healthy, Alan cut an imperious and endearingly eccentric figure. He seldom rode in cars, instead transporting himself over the Santa Cruz hills on a Raleigh three-speed bicycle, riding with such intensity none of my peers on their ten-speeds could keep up. Perfectly capable of haranguing a limousine full of visiting dignitaries for thoughtlessly running over a snake, he was more likely to lend his formidable charm to revealing the wonder of bird, leaf, and beetle to all who would stop and listen.

Alan was the master of that garden. Because he felt so strongly about soil and star, bug and begonia, so did we. His talks always pointed to one thing: the paramount importance of observation, of active study of life in the garden.

Work resumed, one day passed, then another. Morning, high noon, fading evening, cold dark night, and then the warming apricot glow along the horizon again. The rooster and I went once more through our stubborn ritual. People came to admire the garden. We collected tins and baskets of cut flowers and vegetables for a roadside stand, free for the taking. Peacocks strutted and shrieked, doves cooed. (Alan fed them homemade scones.) This weed was no longer rootless. The garden had grown another gardener.

I have met many gardeners since then. One I knew, in the backwoods of Missouri, could neither read nor write but grew all his own food and kept twelve hives of bees, all caught wild, all so gentle he worked without a mask, smoke, or a shirt on his back.

Down the road was another, Millie Keys. Her husband, Bill, liked to fish; Millie had a passion for iris. Every iris that ever won the Dykes Medal grew in Millie's garden. The Keys also had a big vegetable garden, with asparagus, raspberries, and fruit trees in addition to the usual potatoes, corn, and spinach, and they got more out of it than they could eat. Millie could strike a rose cutting under a Mason jar as well as any gardener, Alan included, and her raspberries, grown without sprays, were flawless. She spent no more than an hour or two a day in her garden, but she was there every day. She loved to show me the complex maps and rambling notes she made to keep track of all those irises, which had long since wandered around the hillsides and disappeared into the wild growth nearby.

Wild Raspberries

*W*herever I go, my first interest is the soil. Even in a parking lot I admire the diligence that creates soil in the low shelter of wheelstop curbs. In these protected sanctuaries, the wind lays down fine particles of dust; leaves drift in and stay to slowly decay. In time, weeds spring up to launch a subterranean assault on the asphalt.

On a car trip through the Midwest last summer, I stopped somewhere in Iowa, got out, and walked into a cornfield to see what had become of the fertile plains the pioneers found here. From where I was standing the land was planted in corn for a day's drive in every direction. At my feet, it glistened with recent rain. I stooped and tried to press a finger into the still-moist earth, but even wet it was too hard, too packed by the wheels of huge machines, to allow my finger to penetrate more than a fraction of an inch. No worms worked air and drainage into this dirt. Modern methods produced large stalks of corn, but for every bushel harvested, they let the rain carry off two of soil.

Nearby was a woodlot, one of yesteryear's holdovers. In a ditch along its flank water flowed. The soil here was healthy, alive, laced with the roots of herb and weed. Farther on, under the trees themselves, the mosaic of twig and leaf rustled under my foot, awakening my ear to the presence of others. Birds chattered warnings about the noisy intruder. Squirrels flew to distant branches. Other creatures, unseen, traversed every inch of the woods — microbe, beetle, and cricket moved through the leaves, air, and soil, churning the whole thing like a big, airy compost. In that place, I felt an instinctual sense of belonging, a knowledge that I was home. The cornfield, by contrast, may feed me but it left me uneasy.

That same summer my wife, Dessie, and I went hiking in an Adirondack wood. The area boasts some forty-six peaks exceeding 4,000 feet in altitude; those who climb all of them become "Forty-Sixers." Dessie likes to take me along to carry the pack.

For a while we hiked along John's Brook, listening to the water play against the big black boulders in its path. There are boulders like that everywhere in the Adirondacks, hitchhikers dropped off 12,000 years ago by the great ice sheets that carved out these hills and valleys. Now they lie there, immobile, musing over that ancient journey, slowly vanishing beneath a carpet of gray-green lichen.

Soft, that carpet, but like the weeds in the parking lot, bent on larger ends. Along with the wind, rain, freezing cold, and summer heat, these simple plants (lichens and then mosses) slowly render the giant boulder they cling to into one of earth's most precious treasures: good, rich soil. Slowly they crack their hosts into shards, gravel, and then sand. Always, the searching roots probe deep into the stone, drawing out the precious minerals and transforming them into new life.

In the course of time, lichens are followed by higher

10

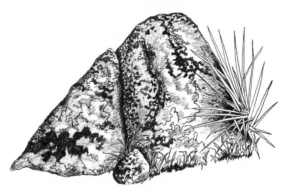

plants. Dust blows into the crevices. Mosses grow and die. These early pioneer plants build a loose protosoil. As it thickens, the deeper roots of annuals and biennial plants find a home. Its loose organic texture stores moisture well and makes a fine seedbed for new seedlings. The roots of the new plants continue to pry cracks in the stone, dividing mineral from mineral. From spring to fall, from seed to flower, the cycle of growth and decay leads, in time, to a living fertility, a lush memory that the cornfield can only faintly recall.

As each successive cycle lives and flourishes in its strength, so each eventually dies, giving way to natural successors. As one plant dies into the seedbed of its successor, mild acids are released that mingle with other forces of decay. The decaying plant bodies add fiber — humus — to the mineral portion of the soil. In death, lichens and weeds return to the elements. As they decay, their organic compounds are released into solution or stored in the humus, later to be taken up by other living bodies. Nitrogen, potassium, and other elements are continuously recycled — held for a living moment or two, then given back again.

Over countless springs and winters, one plant form gives way to another. Eventually taller, deeper-rooted perennials establish themselves, and from that point on, the annuals' days are numbered. As the perennials flourish, they come to monopolize the light, moisture, and nutrients needed for seed germination and growth. In time, the perennials too give way, to woody shrubs, which in turn give way to trees. The transitions of plant succession work toward a climax, a species that cannot be challenged further and which can sustain itself indefinitely. In this place I now stand, it is the tall white pines.

They have been here for some time now. We come to an old bridge, supported by posts made of their timbers. In our terms, the bridge is old, built a good century ago. Crossing it, Dessie and I continue down the road and then turn off onto a wooded path.

In the shade of the pines, the air is brisk and my face is soon flushed with the cold. The coming winter is already caressing the slumbering boulders with a cool touch. My black wool sweater holds warmth and woodsmoke.

From a gardener's point of view, the soil under a pine forest like this one isn't very good. It's too acid because of all the fallen needles. High acidity and cold temperatures limit the number and activity of soil organisms. Lack of life in a soil means slow conversion of needles and other forest matter into humus. Since there is little humus here, snow and rainfall sink through this soil quickly, leaching nutrients downward to the rock below.

We move along, not talking much. There is a strong scent of pine in the air. Gradually, my eyes adjust to the forest shadows. Little grows in the deep shade — lichens and moss, some groups of fern here and there, bunchberries. All huddle together in small colonies. In the odd sunny spot along the path, wood sorrel spreads its carpet.

The path winds along the brook. Up ahead, a lean-to ap-

pears. We reach it quickly. Walking around the campsite, I feel a tentative, furtive curiosity, as if I were poking around in someone's living room. But the gardener in me needs to examine the soil here, so I bend down to dig in it.

Digging gently, I manage to ease up some eight inches of soil. It is fine and crumbly, a rich light brown. Taking a handful, I squeeze it, making a ball that holds the imprint of my fingers — a good sign, since it tells me that this soil retains water well. Now I run my thumb against the ball, and it breaks up into smaller, irregular lumps, like bread crumbs. Another good sign. Soil that has a malleable crumb structure allows air to circulate around the roots. Soil that is too clayey can be pressed into a ball, but it doesn't crumble so freely, if at all. Clay soils don't breathe.

At the other end of the spectrum, soil that is too sandy would crumble and fall apart easily — too easily. It probably wouldn't even hold its shape in the first place. Water runs right through sand, as do air and nutrients. This forest soil in my hand is friable, the good intermediate that gar-

13

deners seek. This soil accepts and releases, has a rhythmic circulation like healthy skin.

The best, most friable soils of all are found under prairies, along river bottoms, and under deciduous, not coniferous, forests. The leaves that fall to earth in a deciduous forest are less acid than pine needles, and the temperatures are normally warmer. More soil microbes and other organisms can live in them to eat, digest, and aerate the soil. Rich in organic material, such soils hold moisture and nutrients well and are superb for farming and gardening. In a forest of oak, for instance, the earth might well attain a rich, deep, chocolate-cake texture. The soil in my hand is better than I expected in an evergreen forest, but still it's too light — more of an angel food.

Living soil breeds life and invites seed germination, root penetration, nutrient manufacture and storage, and the circulation of air and water. Squeezing the ball of soil in my hands once more, I feel the grains of disintegrated rock in it, and images of long nights, cold winds, and misty mornings come to mind. The decaying needles lightly prick my skin. Much time, lots of bacteria, and all the other forces of nature are at work here. In a way, it doesn't matter whether I garden or not, whether I grow one tomato bigger than another. What matters is that I experience nature, that I sense her power.

Breathing the tangy fragrance around us, Dessie and I move on, walking slowly, just glad to be there. Presently my attention is drawn to a break in the shadows up ahead, and to a growing light. The air changes, losing some of its pineyness, taking on a hint of something fresher, greener. Just as I sense this, Dessie says, in a tone of soft surprise, "I smell berries!" *Berries?* I think, *People don't smell berries in the wild; animals — rabbits, deer — do.*

I was wrong. The path bent around another turn, the dark pines gave way to bright-leaved maple and birch, and in a wide, open glade where neither conifer nor deciduous tree ruled was a spreading bramble of red, ripe, delicious raspberries.

According to the logic of plant succession, we shouldn't have found raspberries successfully competing with trees. But fortunately, nature isn't always logical, and there they were. Somehow the trees lost their dominance in this spot, and the raspberries took over.

It wasn't difficult to see why. The key, as always, was under my feet. Beneath the bramble the woodland floor was littered with decomposing, half-charred branches. There had been a fire here, probably caused by lightning, and it had opened the way for the raspberry rebellion. When the smoke had cleared, sunlight had come streaming in. The seeds got the message and decided it was time to wake up and get to work.

But how did raspberry seeds get here in the first place? Like the soil, the earthworm, and the warbler, raspberry seeds are part of the reserves of the forest. Birds feed on the berries elsewhere, then airmail them in. The seeds are indigestible and pass through their bodies. Warmed by the sun, the seeds had sprouted, sending up the first of the long, stickery canes that now make up this wild bramble before me.

That fire was a double blessing, for it also left an added bonus: potash, a valuable source of the nutrient potassium. So these raspberries thrived. Soon their wide-ranging, shallow root system was soaking up the water here, and for a change it was their leaves that were casting the shadows, holding back their competitors.

Raspberries come off the stalk effortlessly into the hand,

rise swiftly to the mouth. *All gardening should be so easy*, I think, popping them down. Now that I know what raspberries like, maybe I'll grow some. They want a humusy soil, slightly acid, and rich in potassium. They want good direct sun and good drainage too. In a garden the fruit would need protection from birds, a net of some kind. To avoid ending up with a tangled bramble like this, they'd need to be trained to a trellis or along wires. I make a mental note to take a look at a gardening manual when I get home to see how they should be pruned.

Only moments earlier some subtle shift in nature's light, color, and scent had spoken to Dessie here, causing her exclamation. She grew up in these woods, and her experiences as a child, of finding wild raspberries here, has stayed with her. But something else happened as well. The relaxed awareness of our walk made us more perceptive of our world. Without meaning to, we let our usual mental chatter drift away, and we were just here, fresh, composed, receptive to what nature had to say to us.

THREE

Seer and Seen

*I*n fact, the link between me and those raspberries runs much deeper than taste. It is a link, however, that does have to do with the senses, specifically with their bright red color and with my ability to perceive it.

These berries are red because they contain a group of chemical substances known as carotenoids — the same substances that, along with xanthophylla and anthocyanin pigment, turn an autumn leaf auburn, butter yellow, pollen gold. Nature is lavish in her production of carotenoids: biologists estimate her annual yield at some 100 million tons. What is most striking about carotenoids, however, is that they are not only responsible for the red of the raspberry, but are also essential to my ability to *see* those berries at all. Without vitamin A, which my body manufactures out of the carotenoids in the food I eat, I would not be able to see any color, or anything at all. "All vision," according to biologist George Wald, "and photoreception is ultimately dependent on carotenoids."[1] And along with vision and pigmentation — seer and seen — carotenoids are also thought to play an important role in our other senses as well — in Dessie's ability to sense the fragrance of those berries, in my ability to relish their flavor.

We are linked to nature in more ways, at more levels, than we consciously know. The scent of the lily, the freshness of the air after a rain shower, the muffled beat of a quail flushed from cover — our experiences are more than passing moments. They are the tapestry of origin and evolution, a tapestry that weaves us as we perceive it.

There was a time when there was no life in this tapestry. It was a time of vast primordial seas laced with chemicals, illuminated by the constant dazzle of unfiltered sunlight and the flash of ancient thunderstorms crackling and booming, sending lances of lightning down into the watery soup below. And then, it is thought, one of those bolts mysteriously catalyzed the change from disparate elements into life.

The first plants to appear were the primitive algaes. They were followed by more complex water-based organisms and, finally, those which in time migrated onto the land. As they developed, plants went from being thin, unrooted, open-pored water dwellers, without any internal systems of support or conduction, to more specialized land dwellers, equipped with an anchoring and feeding root system. They also developed a cuticle, pierced with myriad openings known as "stomata" to allow gas exchange, over most of their surface to keep them from drying out, and a specialized system of channels — xylem and phloem — for transporting water and nutrients. Only much later came those organisms capable of motion but lacking the ability of plants to manufacture their own food: the animals.

In all of these transformations, each taking many thousands of years, nature's method began with abundance. Her

first principle is relentless, extravagant fertility. Allowed to reproduce unchecked for a week, just one of those same primitive algae could *literally* bury the earth. Each year nature sows the air with trillions of pollen grains, collectively weighing millions of tons. Puffball mushrooms release thousands of spores with every raindrop that strikes them for days on end, a gush of procreative vigor. Every dandelion in the lawn sends off hundreds of floating white parachutes that bob and drift through the air.

Go out in your own backyard and turn the soil: in a matter of days you'll find things sprouting there that you've never seen before. They may be weeds, and you may want only to get rid of them, but they are irrefutable evidence of nature's fertility. After World War II, parts of bombed-out London were quickly carpeted with wildflowers long absent from the cityscape. Seared by fire, a forest clearing will soon bloom with new life.

Inextricably mixed up with life is death, the great recycler. That sweet-scented forest seedbed there under the raspberries is also a graveyard. Were I to die there, brown and white threads of fungi and bacteria would soon enshroud my bones. My calcium and phosphorus would rise through the network of roots to nourish the bramble, to form new green strands of stem, leaf, and petal.

Along with abundance goes kaleidoscopic variability, a constant evolutionary juggling of the threads of the tapestry, a kind of cosmic "doodling," as biologist Anthony Huxley puts it. A single bacterium contains about 10 million bits of genetic information. A simple insect, 10 *billion.* Through mutation and sex, nature constantly mixes her messages, trying for new effects. As one thing dies out, many new ones are born. Only the smallest fraction is kept, is woven into the tapestry. The rest are casually, ruthlessly thrown out.

Along with variability goes increasing complexity. The plant kingdom ranges from microscopic bacteria to giant sequoia, from life spans measured in minutes to those lasting thousands of years. Today, there are well over 300,000 kinds of flowering plants in the world.

As it is with plants, so with animals. The clumsy, flapping archaeopteryx has become a multitude of birds, various in the extreme. The tree shrew, our own earliest ancestor, has become mammals innumerable: East Indian tigers, midwestern prairie dogs, furry lemurs in the trees of Madagascar.

Last, in company with abundance, variability, and complexity, comes interdependence. As evolution advances, nature's forms often become more specialized and, as a consequence, more dependent on one another. The weave becomes finer, the threads almost indistinguishable.

Penstemons exemplify the intricacy of the fabric. A wildflower, they are sown by nature's liberal hand all over our continent: every state in the union (except Hawaii) is represented by at least one native penstemon. If the wild turkey should have been our national bird, the penstemon deserves to be our national flower.

Penstemons are hardy, pioneering plants. Given enough sun, they will grow in difficult soils — mountain gravel, high plains "gumbo," even in sand dunes. Indians used penstemon extracts to treat fever, toothache, and whooping cough, and to make a green dye. Penstemons have an urbane side as well. They were an instant hit when first introduced to nineteenth-century English gardeners. William Robinson described forty-five species in *The English Flower Garden*, and Gertrude Jekyll recommended their use in midsummer beds along with snapdragons for spikes of color.

An extremely varied genus, the 250-odd species of penstemon range in size from diminutive alpines to small shrubs, and in color across the spectrum, from whites and yellows to reds and pinks to the predominant blues and purples. The range of form and color found in penstemons hints at the interdependence and the intricacy of the tapestry.

At the turn of the century, when Mrs. Myrtle Hebert was only seven years old, her family moved from Nebraska to a ranch in the foothills of the Big Snowy Mountains of central Montana. They traveled on a train that carried furniture, tools, and livestock as well as passengers. At the end of the line they changed to wagons for the rest of the journey across open country. "Central Montana," Mrs. Hebert recalls, "was then, in 1902, a wildflower paradise. Many of the treasures we saw then have been completely wiped out by cultivation and overgrazing. But that first year aroused in me an interest in wildflowers that has grown over the years." [2]

One birthday, Myrtle Hebert's children gave her a wild-

21

flower identification book. She joined seed exchanges and started writing for a small gardening monthly. When the dust bowl years arrived, and the wind blew away her cultivated flowers, she concentrated on drought-tolerant wildflowers. Gradually, her attention focused on penstemons, and in time she helped found the American Penstemon Society.

Because her husband worked for the railroad, Mrs. Hebert had a free pass, and she made the most of it. She usually took a trowel along on her travels, just in case something special caught her eye, such as this: "*Penstemon albinus* varies greatly, in the wild, from tall scraggly plants with dingy colored off-white flowers, to a delightful form I found in the edge of the Brakes. It was a dwarf, compact, with clear white flowers and just a flush of pink in the throat, and always the conspicuous black anthers like velvet dots." Or this one: "A charming rather dwarf [penstemon of the section] habroanthus, with wee red buds strung like beads along stems that develop into sturdy branches of deep blue bells." [3]

Penstemons have alliances with others besides the gardener. Just as we could not exist without flowers, so they mainly depend on insects for their renewal from generation to generation. The penstemon flower is, in the majority of cases, shaped like a bugle. In evolutionary terms, this is an advanced form. The petals unite to make a tube of the corolla. Frequently the tube has a protuberance, a lower lip, which functions as a landing platform for bees and other pollinators.

The fact that blue is a color bees favor helps explain why that color is popular in the genus: it's an efficient way to advertise. In this case, bees and flowers have evolved a close partnership.

Penstemon strictus

Other penstemons have formed a similar arrangement with hummingbirds, those "glittering fragments of the rainbow," as Audubon dubbed them. Hummingbirds depend largely on flower nectar for energy. Their intense flight is only made possible by a warm-blooded metabolism fueled by a regular supply of concentrated energy. That's the reason for their long bills and extendable tongues, designed to reach deep into a flower to draw up its nectar. Just as the hummingbird's bill has adapted to a particular function, so have these plants evolved in symbiosis with it, developing especially long, tubular blossoms shaped for hummingbird bills.

The forerunners of the hummingbird flowers of North America were originally pollinated by bees and other insects. But some flowers among those blue-dressed blossoms were passed over. Perhaps nature, doodling, had made their corollas unusually long, placing the nectar a little too deeply for bees to easily reach. But one quick, fortuitous probe of the flower by a hummingbird searching perhaps for an insect, and — aha! — the bird had found a new source of sustenance. In the ensuing relationship, the bird and blossom fashioned each other. Were we able to look back over the centuries, we would see them weaving each other, the flowers continuing to draw out the hummer's bill longer and longer, while the birds appeared to select for greater and greater length of corolla. The nectar was hidden ever more secretly from those tedious bees, and eventually the old landing platform itself was discarded. An interbreeding barrier arose — now hummers habitually visit certain penstemon species, while bees visit their special flowers — and so a new species was born in nature.

Along with their form, the flowers slowly changed color as well. Bees, it turns out, do not perceive red. To them the

Penstemon barbatus with rufous hummingbird

Delphinium cardinale, the red columbine, the *Penstemon card-wellii* are just part of life's dull backdrop. Birds, however, *do* see red; in fact, they see more or less the same colors humans do, and to them red stands out vividly. So, said penstemons that once dressed in blue, these birds seem to favor red, so red we'll be. And ever so gradually, with the help of those ubiquitous pigments, that's exactly what happened. Another wall was erected at the interbreeding barrier, dividing species from species.

Looking out the window as I write, I see a magpie flash by, its glossy black and white colors reminding me of a flying spectator shoe. With a harsh caw, it boldly settles in my lawn. Night is falling, and the setting sun throws the nearby mountains into sharp relief, brushing the clouds above with a reddish glow. Lightning flashes, reminding me of ancient origins. It is fall, a season of transience. Like everything else, we emerge for our moment, then sink back into the elemental cycle.

My infant son comes into the room. His fresh skin is smooth and tight. He gurgles unformed words like a fledgling bird trying out its voice. Having just learned to walk, he now plays with this newfound ability, standing precariously

on the bed and diving face-first into the blankets, laughing in his throat over and over again . . . until suddenly he takes an extra bounce and smacks into the wall. A moment's pause, while he absorbs the shock. I hold my breath. Then he laughs. He seems amused by pain, indestructible, full of life. He looks up at me, with simple, full-bodied presence. From the silent past a veil lifts, and for a moment my grandfather's visage, long gone, inhabits his young face.

The world is full of ancestors and descendants. The tapestry continues to weave. Bird and flower, bee and blossom, gardener and garden — this whole strange, intertwined world lives, dies, and lives together.

When I look up again, the magpie is gone. I can see autumn's colors fading as the year moves on toward winter. Heavy with seed, the fields are a rich, rusty brown. The first stars come out, greeting this single human sentience, galaxies away.

From Rice-Making Moon
to Temple of the Sun

*O*ver 100 million years ago, there were no raspberries. In fact, there was no such thing as a flowering plant at all. It was a warmer, wetter world than the one we know today, a world dominated by the dinosaurs. Plants did exist, to be sure, but they were the somber greens of fern and conifer, of those organisms that are reproduced by spore and wind-borne pollen, not by flower. The lush sexuality of the orchid or the rose, the compact energy of grains and legumes, did not yet exist.

Nor did man. In fact the entire class of mammals was represented by nothing more mighty than a small, retiring, rodentlike tree shrew.

But winds of change were blowing. In that world of the reptile and the insect, the evening brought a strange stupor. As the air cooled off at night, those who ruled, from majestic brontosaurus to smallest fly, sank perforce into the metabolic lassitude that all cold-blooded creatures experience when the temperature falls. Dependent on the warmth of their environment, be it air or water, they helplessly wind down like mechanical toys. At night (or in winter), cold-blooded means slow-blooded.

Anathena ellioti, Indian tree shrew

And night was thus the time when our ancient forebear, that tree shrew, ventured out to feed. The mammals of that age were necessarily nocturnal. Like any other warm-blooded animal, including human beings and birds, they had a great advantage in their all-season, round-the-clock quickness of metabolism and mind. Emancipated from external conditions, they could stay alert in the cold.

A price was paid, of course, for this improvement in design. Maintaining a warm-blooded body is like running an engine at a high rpm — it tends to require a concentrated sort of fuel and it burns that fuel up quickly. Compared to the lizards and bugs, we may be quick, but we're not exactly what you would call fuel-efficient.

The tree shrews got by on torpid grubs and insects, feeding by night, hiding in those same conifers by day. Without a change in the menu, without something more suitable to feed a larger, more complex species, mammals would have been unable to find enough energy at night to support evolutionary advances.

But that change came. A somnolent world turned a new trick, and nature created an entirely new category of plant, the angiosperms, a plant that flowers and produces an encased seed, a kind of box lunch to help the new shoot get started. Today, the proteins, sugars, and carbohydrates that fuel our inner fires come mainly, whether directly or indirectly, from the angiosperms, from flowering plants like wheat, rice, corn, and beans, among many others. The immense advantage of a warm-blooded metabolism, of our quick brain and muscles, wouldn't otherwise be possible. The fate of mammals and flowering plants, as Loren Eiseley has pointed out, is closely entwined. We have flourished together.

The better part of human history has been the story of our slowly developing relationship with the angiosperms. Until very recently, that relationship was a discriminating, but nonintensive one. Nature provided; man gathered, or hunted, but did not cultivate. The implications of that change lie at the very heart of our culture.

It was a time of year known to the Ojibwa as *Manominike-gisiss*, the rice-making moon, the month we now call August.[1] The most important event of the year, the autumn hunt, was to begin soon, but first there was something almost as important to attend to: the annual harvest of the wild rice that grew so lushly in the marshy areas along the banks of the nearby river Kakagon, in what we now call Wisconsin.

Rice was a staple of the Ojibwa diet and was used in a

multitude of ways — served with game, boiled with fish, made into a breadlike paste, used to thicken broths, popped like popcorn, and even mixed with such delicacies as cranberries and maple syrup.

In the earliest days of the month, birch-bark canoes were pulled out of the water and carefully inspected for leaks and other damage; during the coming harvest they would be loaded to capacity, over and over again. The sky was watched for signs of bad weather — a storm would be a disaster, blowing all the ripening seed off the stalks before it could be gathered. Bark was stripped from cedar trees around the camp, and its slippery inner layers were fashioned into long cords, which were rolled up and placed near the canoes. The basswood mats on which the rice would be dried were aired in the sun, while the *abwadjigan*, the frameworks that would hold the mats over low drying fires, were built.

All this work was done by the women of the tribe. The men were hunters, not gatherers. They sat and watched, talking among themselves, now and then rising, picking up their weapons, and setting off into the forest for deer and elk or over to the rice fields, a few miles away, to stalk the wildfowl that were always to be found there at that time of the year, lured by the ripening bounty.

It was nearly midmonth when the canoes were ready and the cedar strings prepared. Then the women took these things to the places along the Kakagon where the river widened and slowed, to the marshy spots where the wild rice grew taller than a person, eight or nine feet in the air, as far as the eye could see, in all directions.

Two to a canoe, they set out from the shore. One used a long pole with a forked end to push the craft slowly into the green mass of straight stalks, long flat leaves, and heavy, dropping sprays of seed. Her partner knelt at the opposite end of the canoe and began her task, repeatedly reaching out with one arm, encircling a clump of stalks, and quickly tying it into a bundle with a length of cedar cord. She worked swiftly, surely, with the smooth motions of long experience. Where the boat had passed through, the solid mass was transformed into orderly sheaves, tall, rustling islands dotting the water.

For the next two weeks, nothing more was done. The bound stalks continued to ripen in the sun. Back in camp the women prepared two harvesting sticks, each about a yard long and tapering in diameter from a little over an inch at the widest end to nothing at all at the other. One was perfectly straight, the other curved like a bow.

At the end of the month they returned, for the last time, to the rice fields. Once again they divided into pairs. Again, one woman guided the canoe along the gathering lanes while the other tended to the harvest, catching each sheaf with the curved stick, bending it over the side of the boat, then striking it sharply with the other to dislodge the seed, which fell into a pile in the bottom of the boat. They worked steadily, filling the canoe until one end had settled so low in the water it seemed as if it might slip below the surface of the river at any minute. Then they exchanged tools and tasks and continued on until the other end was just as heavily laden. Periodically they returned to shore and emptied the boat, then set out again.

Once the harvest was in, the next step was to dry the rice on the *abwadjigan* and, finally, to separate the husk from the nutritious kernel. In this last step, a small amount of rice was wrapped in a skin bag, which was placed in a hole in the ground. Then the help of one of the heavier men was enlisted, to tread upon it. The kernels were gleaned from

31

the seeds by opening the bag and tossing it gently in the air to let the wind carry off the lighter husks and other chaff. The kernels were then stored in skin sacks or bark boxes; five bushels was usually enough to see a family through the winter. Along the Kakagon, where the rice fields covered many square miles, each harvest yielded enough rice to feed several thousand Ojibwa.

The life of early man is often portrayed as a desperate, incessant hunt for food, but there is ample evidence that this wasn't necessarily the case, that for most of our 2 million or so years on earth, our species has found nature to be so liberal a provider that we hardly needed to intervene in her processes at all. With virtually no prompting, she furnished us with a nutritious and well-rounded diet, the clothes on our back, our weapons, storage containers, building materials, medicines, and more. Everything we needed was already there, in the leaves, bark, roots, and creatures of the world around us. Moreover, as far as we can tell from what we find in the fossilized garbage heaps of our distant ancestors and from studying the few remaining groups on the earth that still follow the hunter-gatherer way of life, man didn't have to work all that hard to keep his larder well stocked: two or three days a week, on average. The Ojibwa collected all the rice they needed for a full year in a week or two. Lester Brown, a contemporary student of man's relationship with the earth, agrees that, using flint sickles and wooden mortars and pestles, "a prehistoric family working for three weeks of a normal harvest could have acquired about a ton of clean grain, perhaps enough for a year's supply." [2]

Man's view of nature was in all likelihood one in which pragmatism coexisted with awe and reverence. The world that was so fruitful was no doubt also sacred and required special kinds of behavior, actions that would not only appease the gods, but also complement natural processes. When, for example, the prehistoric gatherer unearthed a wild yam, we know that she was careful to immediately cut its top off and put it back in the ground, not only to propitiate the spirits that had put it there in the first place, but also to ensure that it would be replaced. (The yam is a plant that regenerates vegetatively, from portions of the full-grown plant rather than from seed.) In the same way, she also avoided disturbing certain other plants once they had flowered, because to do so would be a sacrilege and would also, not incidentally, disrupt their seed production.

Thus man observed nature, learned her ways, and acquired a reliable and timeless tradition of knowledge about how to live in the world. He came to understand that some plants do better in the open sun, while others prefer shade; that some need lots of water, while others can do with less;

that the well-manured, loosened earth of a rubbish heap invites more vigorous growth than the hard, sun-baked clay of the open range.

Of course, the hunter-gatherer way of life had its limitations too, and man was bound by those as well. He had to live as a nomad, never staying in one place too long. More important, his numbers had to be kept low — there were probably never more than 10 million of us in the entire world at any one time before the advent of agriculture.

Then, over thousands of years, a subtle but profound change took place. Man the hunter-gatherer slowly turned into man the farmer. Motivated by our insatiable curiosity, we began to find new ways to put all the lore acquired during millennia of living with nature to work for us. We began to deliberately intrude in natural processes, in order to make nature even more fruitful, and more reliably so. We began to domesticate animals, first sheep and goats, then pigs, and finally cattle and horses, turning as we did from hunter-gatherers to herdsmen. We began to deliberately remove plants that competed with those we favored, thus inventing the weed. We scratched crude ditches in the ground to divert streams, thus inventing irrigation. And, most crucial of all, we grasped the secret behind the mystery of how new plants grow from old ones and began to save and sow seed.

Thus the cultivation of nature — agriculture — was born, about 10,000 years ago, in the Middle East, in Central America, and in Southeast Asia, setting in motion a cultural revolution whose effects went far beyond our simple attempts to tame nature. For with agriculture came food surpluses, for the first time in our history. With those surpluses came liberation from the nomadic way of life, the opportunity to settle in one place for good, the opportunity for more and more members of our species to do something other than look for food. The very seeds of a modern civilization made up primarily of those who do other things than produce food, who live in dense clusters, whose numbers strain at the limits of our ability to feed ourselves, a world whose natural environment is now sorely tried by us — all this arose in response to our turn from hunting and gathering to herding and farming.

Within a remarkably short period of time — 7,000 years or so — we had succeeded in domesticating the angiosperms we live on today, with the exception of tomatoes and coffee, which are of more recent cultivation. Of them all, wheat and rice are today by far the most important food sources for us, providing over half of our calories each day.

Most of the food we now eat comes from a relatively few, highly cultivated crops, a mere handful of the more than 300,000 flowering species that exist on this planet. We still gather, mainly nuts, mushrooms, herbs, algae, maple syrup, and, yes, wild rice, but most of what we consume is planted, tended, and harvested by man alone and would disappear if we did. In a few instances, both wild and domesticated varieties can be found, and sometimes the former, like wild raspberries, are more highly prized, but these are now very much the exceptions. Similarly, the ancient gathering ways still persist in a few isolated parts of the world, with all their original simplicity, directness, and freedom. Remarked an Australian aborigine a decade or so ago:

You people go to all that trouble, working and planting seed, but we don't have to do that. All these things are there for us, the Ancestral beings left them for us. In the end, you depend on the sun and rain just as we do, but the difference is we just have to go and collect the food when it is ripe. We don't have all this other trouble.[3]

One of the more intriguing things about agriculture is the remarkable way in which nature responded to man's attempts to domesticate her. As we began to select for certain plants and certain traits, and to cultivate those more intensely, she in turn adapted with uncanny appropriateness. First, the whole plant grew larger, thus more productive. Even more striking, however, is the fact that at the same time, the specific part of the plant of interest to its human cultivators — whether pod, root, fruit, or flower — grew proportionally larger than the plant as a whole did, as if nature understood precisely what was needed. Not only that, but the net yield, measured by weight, increased. Even in a plant like the domesticated tomato, which bears fewer fruits than its wild relatives, the size of each tomato increased so dramatically that the overall yield went up. And in plants like apples, pears, and cherries, the number and size of the seeds simultaneously decreased, further increasing the yield of the parts consumed by man, the flesh and pulp.

In some plants, like peas, the pod migrated toward the top of the plant, as if to make harvesting easier. Seeds that in nature germinate and mature at different times, to increase the chances of surviving a disease or spell of inclement weather, were replaced by seeds that germinated all at once, thus allowing crops that sprouted, grew, and ripened all at the same time, rather than in staggered intervals.

In many cases the life span of the cultivated plant decreased sharply, making it possible for early farmers to sow, raise, and harvest two or three crops in the same amount of time, from the same area of land, that had been required for one before. Cultivated plants lost whatever bitter taste, toxicity, or mechanical means of protection — thorns, prickles, etc. — they may have evolved and that their wild cousins may retain to this day to defend themselves against predators. In some cases, a plant found its relationship with man to be of great evolutionary advantage: together, we formed a union more powerful than either could have achieved on its own.

Wheat is a good example. Wild species of wheat tend to develop seed heads that "shatter," that is, that easily break apart and cast the seeds to the ground. This trait is an admirable one in nature, where it helps perpetuate the species, but is highly undesirable in agriculture since it greatly complicates harvesting. Early farmers selected those occasional wheat plants that showed a tendency to produce a nonshattering head. This is now a prominent feature in all domesticated types of wheat.

Farming itself evolved as well. Early man was not, despite his very significant achievements, all that good a farmer. He often made serious mistakes, like allowing his stock to overgraze pastures, thus destroying the cover crops that held the soil in place and causing erosion. He didn't always understand that the fertility of the soil could be depleted. The fires he set to clear the land also eradicated the tree cover, altering the microclimate and transforming lush, fertile acres into desert. We had to keep learning, through many thousands of years of trial and error, the ways in which we could live in harmonious interdependence with the land. Where we did, we developed truly great agricultural civilizations, based on sound and sustainable practices, practices we can still learn from today.

One such culture emerged in the New World, but not in North America, the land of the Ojibwa and others, where the game and wild produce were often so abundant there was little need to make nature work harder. Instead, it appeared in harsher regions thousands of miles to the south,

37

up and down the western length of South America, where a number of separate tribes were slowly converging to form what would become one of the highest cultures of the earth ever known, that of the Incas. To this day we are greatly indebted to the Incas, for "more than half of the foods that the world eats today were developed by these Andean farmers," [4] including strawberries, pineapples, peanuts, corn, potatoes, tomatoes, and many varieties of bean, chocolate, and squash.

Inca culture was in full flower when the first white men arrived in the New World, some four centuries ago. As a model for living with the land, cultivating it intensively, and yet steadily enhancing rather than depleting it, it has never been surpassed.

The Inca Empire first rose to prominence in the twelfth century, in and around what is now Cuzco, Peru. A mere 400 years later, when it was first encountered by Europeans, it encompassed some 8 million subjects, extended 2,500 miles along the western length of South America, and included some 400,000 square miles of what is now Bolivia, Ecuador, Chile, Argentina, and Peru.

The strength of the Inca Empire lay in its relationship to the land. It was based, as all such cultures are, on two things: respect for the soil and appreciation for natural diversity. There were earlier cultures in these same areas — the Chavin, the Nazca, the Tiahuanaco, the Mochica, among others — and they had made some agricultural progress, domesticating certain varieties of maize and building modest irrigation systems in a few scattered places. But these cultures had remained limited to the population that could be supported by the rich soil at the bottom of the numerous small river valleys that run from the Andes down to the Pacific. The single most critical factor enabling the Incas to rise above all these fragmented, localized cultures and consolidate them into an empire was their creation of arable land.

The terrain in this part of South America falls into three or four general zones. Much of the coast is barren and dry, suitable only for cultivation of such drought-tolerant crops as cotton, and even then requiring some irrigation. Next are the foothills, characterized mainly by steep slopes. Third is the great sierra itself, the high mountains of the Andes, rising miles in elevation. Above 15,000 feet agricultural planting is usually thought to be impractical due to the lack of moisture and the bitter cold. Finally, on the eastern slope of the Andes begin the hot, wet jungles and the headwaters of the great rivers that flow eastward across the breadth of the continent to the Atlantic. In various parts of their empire the Incas successfully cultivated all these zones.

At the heart of their achievement is the technique of terracing. An ancient method of turning hilly land into flat, arable spaces, terracing has arisen spontaneously in many parts of the world, but rarely has this art realized the scale and perfection it did at the hands of the Incas. Using large blocks of limestone, they cut, polished, and fabricated yard-thick walls, without the use of cement or mortar and with such precision that to this day the blade of a penknife cannot be slipped between their stones. They were able to sculpt the earth, transforming steep slopes into a series of giant shelves, many rising thousands of feet, from as wide as three hundred feet at the bottom to as narrow as three feet at the top. The earth that filled each step was cut out of the hill itself, then steadily enriched and fertilized. Terrace-making was so important to the Incas that the profession was one of the few exempted from the military and public service required of all other able-bodied males.

Their ability to create new land area would have meant

much less, however, if the Incas had not also understood the importance of developing and maintaining its fertility, and this they also did, with equally great skill. First, they made a discipline of returning to the soil every bit of plant material they did not consume, something that many gardeners do today through the practice of composting. Once a crop had been harvested, the stubble was set afire and burned to the ground, providing a rich source of potash for the next year. Those parts of a plant discarded during the preparation of meals were saved and buried. Knowing that maize is a crop that is particularly hard on the soil, draining it of nutrients, while legumes, by contrast, help restore nitrogenous compounds to the earth, the Incas made a practice of interplanting beans among their corn crops, allowing the vines to grow up the stalks.

Second, they made extensive use of manures, mainly the seabird droppings known as guano, also an excellent source of nitrogen. In fact, guano was held in such esteem among the Incas that "to kill a sea bird was a capital offence."[5] (The large deposits of guano along the western coast of South America were mined and exported for centuries, until they were displaced by artificial fertilizers.)

Other forms of manure were also used by the Incas, including human wastes and those of the only animal they domesticated, the llama. The American Indian custom of sowing a fish head in each hole along with two or three corn seeds was probably learned from the Incas.

With land area and fertility assured, only one more thing was needed to firmly establish the Inca Empire as a classic example of sustainable agriculture: a steady, adequate supply of fresh water. In theory, water was abundantly available in the form of the perpetual snows that capped the nearby mountain peaks and in the rivers that coursed from them down to the sea. The only problem was distribution. Here again the Inca genius for agricultural engineering asserted itself. In this case the innovation, one that had also appeared in earlier, minor ways in the region, was irrigation. Like the Romans, whose empire theirs resembled in a number of ways, the Incas became expert at building and maintaining elaborate aqueducts.

Like their terrace walls, the Inca irrigation canals were carved out of the earth and then lined with unmortared, perfectly fitted blocks of stone. Huge channels, twelve feet square in some cases, served as main arteries, carrying water hundreds of miles. Smaller capillaries then branched out into the fields, provided with sluice gates for flow control. Each of these smaller canals led to the top of a terrace system. From its opening, water was released in an even, controlled manner so that it flowed across the shelves of earth, slowly soaking in. In addition to moisture, the Inca irrigation system is thought to have contributed to soil fertility by carrying mineral-rich silts and muds down from higher elevations and settling them out into the cultivated terraces. It all worked so well that regions that would have been naturally dry for half the year were continuously cultivated.

Based on this foundation of soil wealth, the Inca culture was able to accomplish what any society must if it is to flourish: it produced a reliable agricultural surplus, in the form of dried potatoes, quinoa grain, meats, and other goods. Most of the surplus was stored in government granaries all over the empire and was used to alleviate famine and to allow certain members of Inca society to specialize — to become metalworkers, soldiers, terrace designers. The empire, by all accounts, was a stable and benevolent one, a kind of "imperial communism," as it has been called. Like Rome, it was an expansionist culture, one of great military as well as agricultural prowess. Neighboring tribes were methodically subjugated by the Incas. While being allowed to retain the trappings of their own cultural identity, they were also required to swear fealty to the Inca emperor, to revere the Sun God (the supreme Inca deity) above all others, and to consent to follow the Inca system of communal land tenure and mandatory public service.

In the world of the Inca, there was no such thing as private property. All lands and livestock were held in common. Labor and yields were distributed by dividing all arable land into 150- by 300-foot plots called *"topos."* Each *topo* was then assigned to the church, the government, a family, or an individual. Every year all the church lands were worked first, then the government plots, and finally the land belonging to the general populace. Special *topos* were assigned to the elderly, the sick, widows, and those exempted from farming because of their profession, and these were also worked in common. When the size of a family changed, through birth or death, land was added to or subtracted from the family's allotment.

The cycle of working the land began each year in August, at about the same time the Ojibwa were harvesting their rice. It began with a celebration in which the emperor turned the first earth with a golden digging stick. When the celebration ended, work began in earnest. Using their own individual digging sticks, called *"tacclas,"* lines of men slowly worked their way across the field, chanting and loosening the earth as they moved. Following them came a line of women, each equipped with a hoelike implement called a *"lampa,"* used to further break up the larger clods of earth into a fine surface tilth. Finally, a second line of women made its way across the prepared field, dibbling open holes at regularly spaced intervals and dropping in seeds and perhaps a fish head or two for good measure. The act of planting seed was always performed by women.

September was the time to sow corn. October was a

43

month of rest, because that was when the heavy rains came. Other vegetables were planted in November, and potatoes in December. (Remember, the seasons are reversed in the Southern Hemisphere.) Then the fields were irrigated, weeded, and protected from pests and predators until May, when the corn crop was harvested. Three months later, potatoes were collected, and then the fields were allowed to lie fallow for a month or two. Though all this work was done without the aid of draft animals, the life of the Inca farmer was by no means one of incessant toil: the Inca calendar included almost 160 holidays; the average farmer worked no more than four days a week.

Different crops were grown at different elevations. The dry, desertlike western coastal areas were devoted mainly to sweet potatoes, cotton, sugar cane, and gourds. On the lusher eastern slopes of the Andes, peanuts, pineapples, tropical fruits, and cacao were raised. In the more temperate zones up to about 8,500 feet or so, squash, chili peppers, tomatoes, avocados, and many kinds of beans were planted. A wide variety of maize was raised in all zones, up to about 13,000 feet, along with potatoes, including a special frost-tolerant type that could be grown as high as 15,000 feet. Another high-altitude crop favored by the Incas was quinoa, a hardy, protein-rich grain that was ground into a flour and eaten like oatmeal.

Maize, the staple of Inca agriculture, was a crop whose cultivation they excelled in. Over twenty varieties were grown, and some achieved astounding proportions, reaching as high as eighteen feet, with "ears between four and ten inches long, the grains themselves as large as a pea, and the ears on a single plant very numerous."[6] Inca agriculture was also characterized by a sophisticated appreciation for the fundamental importance of natural diversity. They cultivated some forty to fifty kinds of potato and every type of bean known today, with the exception of soy and fava. This emphasis on diversity was a deliberate way of ensuring that overreliance on one or two varieties of a crop would not render the Incas vulnerable to sudden devastation caused by disease or pest. According to Wendell Berry, it is an emphasis that can still be observed in descendants of the Inca. Berry describes the cultivation of as many as fifty wild and semidomesticated types of potato in the areas bordering the plots of contemporary farmers in the Andes. The purpose, says Berry, is this: "If an Andean farmer loses a crop because of an extremity of the weather or an infestation of insects or disease, he may find a new variety that has survived the calamity and produced in spite of it. If he finds such a plant, he may add it to his collections of domesticated varieties or substitute it for one that has failed." [7]

There was also another kind of wealth beneath the earth in the land of the Incas, one that inspired a very different kind of excitement than the reverence they felt for the soil, and one that was to prove their downfall. The Inca Empire was fabulously rich in precious metals, particularly gold and silver. For the Incas, these substances were primarily of artistic value. The glow of gold, which they called "tears of the sun," was mainly a symbol of their primary deity, and they worked it with great skill, fashioning ornaments for the emperor, his retinue, the priesthood, and the adornment of official buildings. Probably the best example of the Inca attitude about these metals is found in "Coricancha," the Temple of the Sun. Coricancha was the emperor's private, enclosed garden, and it was, above all, a paean to the fertility of the soil. Its walls were lined with gold and its thatched roof gleamed with straws of gold. In it stood twenty llamas and their shepherds, all of solid gold, a fountain of gold, and golden trees bearing golden fruit. But the heart of Cori-cancha, and of the empire itself, was its crop of golden ears of corn, boasting tassels of spun gold that waved in the breezes, rising on stalks of pure silver from a plot of "soil" made of golden nuggets. The Incas used golden objects as a way of expressing their devotion to their real wealth, the earth itself.

Others, however, did not share this view. In 1532 Francisco Pizarro entered the land of the Inca accompanied by fewer than 200 conquistadores determined to find and plunder the Incas' incredible mineral wealth. On November 16 of that year, Pizarro was brought into the presence of the Inca emperor Atahuallpa, who received him sitting on a low stool made of solid gold. After a perfunctory greeting, Pizarro's men attacked Atahuallpa's bodyguards, overcame them, and took the emperor prisoner.

Atahuallpa quickly realized that the only thing the bearded strangers were interested in was the tears of the sun, and offered an exchange: in return for his freedom, he would give them a roomful of gold, plus twice as much silver. Pizarro readily agreed, and for the next month a steady stream of Incas arrived bearing gold ingots, most of which had been created by melting down works of art. When the room was full, Pizarro had Atahuallpa put to death. The small part of the treasure that Pizarro sent to Charles V was worth, in current terms, hundreds of millions of dollars and represented more gold than had previously existed in all of Europe. Among the gold ingots borne into the Spanish court were a few forlorn ears of golden corn from Corican-cha. Rumors, of course, persist to this day of treasures hidden from the Spaniards, of golden birds perched on lustrous boughs in cool, dark caverns deep in the Andes, far from the kingdom of the sun.

PART TWO

Garden Masters

The Lineage of the Lawn

*T*he Arkansas River flows sinuously through Riverside Park in Wichita, Kansas. Upstream, at the high school, I learned canoeing. In the park itself, I played ball on broad grass fields, picnicked with my family underneath patriarchal oaks and elms, rode the big swing to its limits, and ran hide and seek through the wild woodlot. I loved the place and thought of it as grand and ancient, somehow left over from another time. Indians, I knew, had camped there.

It's hard now to distinguish my boyish enthusiasm for Riverside Park from my grown-up appreciation for its art. For that is what the great ordinary parks of this country are: works of art. They are not just remnants of nature, passed over in the rush of city growth. They were planned and planted by citizens who belong to a great horticultural tradition, one that shaped the way not only our parks but even our yards are made today.

The greatest of these American park makers, perhaps the only one whose name is widely known, was Frederick Law Olmsted. Olmsted was born on April 26, 1822, in what was then the village of Hartford, Connecticut. He too formed fond memories, playing in the woods, meadows, and rivers near his home. But his park was not delimited, as mine was, by Murdock Avenue, Thirteenth Street, and Riverside Drive. Olmsted had the whole of the New England countryside to roam through.

On long, solitary walks, he explored the rivers and valleys around Hartford. His father enjoyed taking the family on trips by coach and canal boat to view natural scenery. They breathed the bracing air of the White Mountains, traveled the Maine coast, and wandered through the Adirondack forests. It was the age of Emerson and Thoreau, when people turned to nature for their health, both physical and spiritual.

The America that Olmsted knew as a boy and young man was still a profoundly rural nation, but that fact was destined to change dramatically within his lifetime. At his birth, only one in every ten Americans lived in a town of more than 8,000 residents. The population of New York City was a mere 123,000. By the time of his death, in 1903, New York was home to 4 million people.

Like many great gardeners, Olmsted was good at a lot of things. He sailed to China, tried his hand at progressive farming, and helped edit and publish cultural magazines, including *The Nation*. After touring England, he wrote an account of her people, agriculture, and landscape parks entitled *Walks and Talks of an American Farmer in England*. He also walked and talked in the antebellum South, in the years just preceding the Civil War, and his books about that experience were widely read here and abroad by those seeking to understand the coming conflict.

These varied experiences of farming, travel, and writing, though often unsuccessful as business ventures, combined happily in 1857 when a member of the New York City

Parks Commission encouraged Olmsted to apply for the job of superintending work on a park just then being created in the middle of the city. Accepting the challenge, Olmsted was to prove himself a brilliant and tireless administrator, with a strong sense of landscape beauty and a persuasive pen.

The Central Park site was not, in 1857, the graceful composition of meadow, lake, and woods that we see now, needing only the addition of pathways, terraces, and benches to make it complete. Instead, rocky outcroppings of Manhattan schist had ruled out the development of housing. Squatters' huts, pig sties, and slaughter-yard effluvia were the dubious evidence of civilization. The unsanitary conditions of a large swamp had city officials concerned.

Olmsted joined forces with a talented English architect, Calvert Vaux, and together they submitted an improved design for the park, one they called "The Greensward." Their plan envisioned a place where city residents could find fresh air and the scenic pleasures of a country setting, near at hand. "Greensward" was accepted, and in their hands Central Park slowly became, in the midst of urban bustle, one of the best-known islands of natural beauty in the world, one that set a standard of stately trees, smooth turf, and border shrubs softening the hard cityscape nearby, a standard that has influenced American taste in parks — and backyards — ever since. Anyone who has sat on a porch looking out across a groomed lawn into a tree or two spreading its cool canopy of shade, or who has strolled along the turf, clusters of tree and shrub, winding paths, and still ponds or lively brooks of a public park knows the effect of this influence.

Imagine, if you will, entering Central Park of a spring day, by the Students' Gate at 67th Street and Fifth Avenue.

Taking the stroller's lane, you head into the park and toward the new playground. The first thing you do is take a deep breath and relax, no longer on guard about being run over. That is the first great device that Olmsted and Vaux introduced into park design: separate routes for various forms of traffic — in their day, buggies, horses, and people on foot. And where those routes inevitably crossed, they provided tunnels and bridges to maintain the separation.

In the distance to the left is the Dairy, where in Olmsted's time children were given fresh milk. A short walk from Willowdell Arch will take you to the wide promenade under the leafy arch of the mall. As the view opens out at the end of this shade tunnel, you see fellow citizens around the Terrace and Bethesda Fountain. This park, whose walks and views afford a feeling of natural tranquillity, is also a social place. Olmsted firmly believed in the ability of nature to unite people.

From the Terrace, the view across the lake invites investigation in several directions. To the north, high on a hill, Belvedere Castle attracts the curious. Taking the path to the left, you soon glimpse the graceful curve of Bow Bridge, leading you across the water and into the Ramble. This feeling of taking a journey is another basic element in Olmsted-Vaux designs: a sequence of views and other visual invitations draws you on, into a refreshingly contemplative experience.

In Olmsted's day, after crossing Bow Bridge, you would descend into the Ramble, a wild, quiet, solitary woodland in the heart of New York City, where birds gathered in unexpected variety. Lovers would gather here also, to share an alcove bench and talk. Today, only the brave, foolish, or well-protected enter such an isolated place in New York City. Most hold to the upper edge of the lake.

As a young man, Olmsted studied progressive farming by attending Benjamin Silliman's agricultural lectures at Yale. Attracted to country life, in 1846 he signed on as an apprentice to George Geddes, whose farm at Camillus, New York, had been named the best managed in the state. It was during these years that Olmsted also came into contact with the nation's leading agriculturalist and landscape planner of that era, Andrew Jackson Downing, and his journal, *The Horticulturalist*. In fact, it was at Downing's house on the Hudson River where Olmsted and Vaux first met.

With his father's financial help, Olmsted had soon purchased a farm of his own, first at Sachem's Head, up the Long Island Sound, and then a larger, better-situated place called Southfield, on Long Island. At Southfield, he directed a large vegetable and nursery business. Fruit trees, especially pears, were his specialty. Ever industrious, Olmsted was soon active in the local agricultural society, busy laying out his place in the new "natural" style of English estates,

53

and winning a silver spoon for the quality of his produce.

But all this was still some years before his triumph with Central Park, and he was restless, feeling that he had not yet found his true calling. He wanted to see Europe and examine English agricultural practices and landscape-making firsthand. Moreover, he was by then an established man of letters, so when the opportunity came to travel and publish his observations, he put Southfield in the hands of a caretaker and left, sailing for England on April 30, 1850.

Although this trip represented Olmsted's first chance to set eyes on the English landscape parks he had heard so much about, the park that impressed him most was not one of the famous private estates, symbols of wealth and privilege. Instead, when he disembarked at Liverpool and went into a bakery shop, the proprietor directed him to a new park, called "People's Park," at Birkenhead, just across the river.

There Olmsted encountered 125 acres of one of the first public parks in England. Begun in 1844, its creator had "dug a lake and, with the earth taken from it, varied the level surface with artful naturalness; he had created shady glens, open meadows dotted with trees, rock gardens, cricket and archery grounds, ornamental buildings, avenues of trees; and he had made the whole accessible by good hard roads and foot paths. Birkenhead citizens of every class flocked there to pass leisure hours in restful surroundings — invalids, nurses and mothers with children, whole families on holidays, freely enjoying their own park, paid for out of their own tax money." [1]

So taken was Olmsted with the idea of a *public* park that he was moved to write: "Five minutes of admiration and a few more spent in studying the manner in which art had been employed to obtain from nature so much beauty and I was ready to admit that in democratic America there was nothing to be thought of as comparable with the People's garden. Indeed, gardening had here reached a perfection that I had never before dreamed of." [2] In a glowing report to *The Horticulturalist,* he expressed the fervent hope that such a park would be made in America. Unaware of it himself, Olmsted was preparing for a profession not then recognized in the United States, that of landscape architect.

As important to Olmsted as the democratic spirit in which People's Park had been created was the fact that it was a work of art. In England and on the Continent, gardening was considered an artistic endeavor, one whose traditions reached back to classical antiquity. The natural style of the English landscape parks that Olmsted was encountering had arisen in the eighteenth century, in connection with the neoclassical and, later, the romantic movements in art and literature. In gardening, this new style had meant forsaking the straight line and embracing the curve: in the natural style, a stream, a lake with gracefully curving banks, or a serpentine river lies at the foot of gently rounded hills marked by soft groupings of tree and shrub. Typically, a broad lawn extends far into the distance, where it merges with meadow and field.

Stourhead, in Wiltshire, England, is the landmark example of this style. Begun in about 1744 by banker Henry Hoare, Stourhead is a landscape journey for the body and mind. Viewing Stourhead involves taking a circular walk around the lake, a tour that presents successive views of lakeside woods in which replicas of the Pantheon and other neoclassical references periodically appear.

The new style grew out of a cultured desire to look to nature for direction, rather than imposing on her, rigidly and geometrically. The underlying impetus for the natural style — and its most emblematic statement — was a strong interest in discovering and abiding by the "genius of the place," a phrase given us by the poet Alexander Pope, who himself created a well-known garden at his Twickenham estate. The idea is worthy of respect today. Whether the site is that of a small vegetable garden or an 840-acre urban park, the gardener needs first of all to be open to its natural characteristics. Ironic as it may seem, given Olmsted's forceful temperament, he was above all receptive when first surveying a new site. He took an unqualified look, and only when he understood the essence of the place did he make a design that flowed from its inherent potential.

By the time of Olmsted's visits to England, Stourhead was a century old. The classical themes of the garden estates had by then been largely replaced by the "picturesque" — craggy rocks, rustic huts, handmade bridges, and quaint ponds. But the aim remained the same: to make the visitor feel inspired by and alive to nature, to demonstrate that nature can be cultivated as art, and that the cultivator, mankind, belongs in nature.

As rewarding as Central Park was for Olmsted, it was also exhausting. At one point, he had 4,000 men working for him, many of whom had gotten their jobs because of political favoritism. The budget for the park was $8 million at a time when gardeners were paid $1.25 a day. The responsibilities were enormous, the entanglements never-ending.

Under Olmsted's determined hand, the site changed dramatically between 1858 and 1861. Tens of thousands of trees were planted yearly, and more shrubs and vines. Earth and rock that had last been shaped by glacial ice was landscaped with pick and shovel. Out of a miasmal, useless piece of ground arose a park the city could be proud of.

New Yorkers began flocking to it even before it was officially opened, to skate, walk, picnic, and ride. All around its periphery, land values shot up. Central Park made Olmsted's name famous.

At that point, however, the Civil War broke out. As it loomed, Olmsted's books about the South were even more widely circulated. His humanitarian outlook, as well as his practical success in managing Central Park's development, brought his name to the attention of influential men concerned about providing medical support for the ill-organized Union Army.

In 1861, Olmsted took temporary leave of his park duties to become Executive Secretary of the United States Sanitary Commission, forerunner of today's Red Cross. Working feverishly, he began to build a medical supply and relief organization. On April 12 of that year, Confederate artillery fired on federal ships attempting to resupply Fort Sumter, and the war commenced.

Working day and night, assisted by equally energetic and capable colleagues, Olmsted managed to again bring order out of chaos over the next two years. But in doing so he brought himself to the edge of exhaustion, and was from that time on plagued by chronic insomnia. Political infighting also dogged his footsteps: he was too headstrong for the Commission's Executive Committee, and they too interfering for him. After two years of success and exertion, Olmsted desperately needed a change. Forty-one years old, still in debt to his father, with an income that had not for years been adequate to support his family, let alone reduce his debts, he was ready for something different. When a group of investors offered him the job, at many times his Commission salary, of overseeing the Mariposa Mining

Company in California, Olmsted hesitated but briefly before resigning his appointment and sailing for the West Coast in 1863.

Unfortunately, it took him only a little more than a year to determine that the mining operation was located at the wrong end of the mother lode and had no future. During that short time, however, he made enough money to repay his debts, as well as to send some gold home and to make some fruitful investments in California. It was also at this time that the glories of nearby Yosemite caught Olmsted's attention during several camping trips there. Taking an early role in the embryonic conservation movement, he wrote a long report urging the state to save the area from private speculators by making it a public preserve, and later fought for the protection of Niagara Falls and the Adirondacks as well.

As the Mariposa venture was winding down, Vaux wrote to say that they had been offered an opportunity to continue their work on Central Park. Moreover, Vaux had been commissioned to create another design for Prospect Park, in Brooklyn. They could not only resume their old project, but begin a new one, on a better site. Olmsted hesitated, then accepted.

In the few years that he had been gone, Olmsted's reputation had continued to increase, and he soon had more work than he could handle. He and Vaux were commissioned to make numerous parks in New York State and elsewhere. Though they continued to work together, it was clear that Olmsted had become the more well known of the two, and he began working with other architects as well, such as Henry H. Richardson, in a design for Staten Island. In 1873, Olmsted and Vaux decided to dissolve their historic partnership, and from then on Olmsted worked independently.

In the following years, Olmsted went from success to success. While his name is chiefly associated with Central Park, he also designed and landscaped scores of parks, parkways, suburbs, institutions, campuses, and estates throughout North America, from Atlanta to Montreal, and California to New York. Some of the more notable creations he was involved in include Riverside, Morningside, Prospect, and Fort Greene parks in New York City and Brooklyn; South Park and Jackson Park in Chicago; and Mont Royal in Montreal. He helped plan the 1893 World's Columbian Exposition in Chicago and laid out suburbs and subdivisions in Riverside, near Chicago; Brookline, Massachusetts, where he later made his home; Buffalo; and Atlanta. He also helped develop the enormous Vanderbilt estate, Biltmore, at Asheville, North Carolina, in collaboration with architect Richard Morris Hunt. Olmsted also designed the "Emerald Necklace," a string of interconnected parks in Boston, as well as landscaping hospitals, state capitols, and the terrace and grounds of the western side of the U.S. Capitol in Washington, D.C. He was extremely prolific; the amount of work that passed through his office is remarkable.

In 1878, Olmsted tired of the hustle and hard knocks of New York and moved to Brookline, outside Boston. In the two decades since its inception, his office had grown from two to forty employees.

By 1887, Olmsted was at work on a project in California for railroad tycoon, land speculator, and former governor Leland Stanford. Stanford wanted to build a university on a site in Palo Alto, south of San Francisco, in memory of his recently deceased son, who had liked to ride his horse there. Campuses at Yale, Cornell, Harvard, and elsewhere were shaped, in part, by Olmsted's hand. Stanford wanted the campus to be fashioned after the New England model that Olmsted was by then an acknowledged master of.

The site, however, was a windswept, dry, grassland plain, fully exposed to the hot California summer sun. Olmsted was quick to realize that the New England style was not the genius of this place. As he put it, "The absurdity of seeking good pastoral beauty in the far West is more and more manifest." [3] It is a testament to both his talent and his determination that Olmsted did not simply acquiesce to the wishes of his powerful and wealthy client, but instead argued successfully for a very different approach, modeled on Mediterranean examples.

In this plan, the buildings are low one- and two-story structures with tile roofs and Romanesque pillars, arches, and loggias. For appropriate plant selections, Olmsted dispatched a young assistant, Henry S. Codman, to Spain, Greece, and North Africa to find species that would be suited to the Palo Alto climate. Water conservation was encouraged through the use of paving blocks in the central courtyard, rather than the predictable and inappropriate turf. Palms were planted for shade and their tolerance for drought, and also because Olmsted was at that point in his career fascinated with tropical effects. Like the open, grassy areas of a New England campus, the central enclosed courtyard at Stanford has a sense of quiet spaciousness. Around the quadrangle of inward-facing buildings is an arcade, protected from the wind, joining courtyard and structure. The overall feeling is that of an interior oasis, conducive to the same reflective mood apparent in Central Park's Ramble, but achieved with very different elements.

Knowing that Stanford intended the campus to grow, Olmsted planned for future development along the north-south axis of the central quadrangle. In addition, he initiated an arboretum and forest-planting area on the land surrounding the central campus area. His nurseryman, T. H. Douglas, began propagating native plants and specimens from similar habitats around the world for trials under local

Frederick Law Olmsted

In 1860, Olmsted wrote some general instructions to his gardeners about planting trees and shrubs. They are still applicable today, and sum up the way I plant small trees in my own practice.

To plant a tree like Olmsted did:

1. "Every fiber of the root should, if possible, be preserved."

2. "Roots [should be] protected from the sun and wind and frost." Transplanting should be done quickly. Don't let roots dry out.

3. "Cut clean any bruised or broken part of the roots." Damaged roots invite disease.

4. Dig a hole "twice the diameter of the body of the roots."

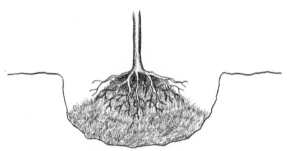

Tree in planting hole

5. "Work industriously, but do not try to plant rapidly."

6. Loosen the ground around the planting hole. This helps the roots grow out of the soil around the root ball and into the surrounding earth.

7. "Roots must be opened and spread out with the fingers upon a bed of carefully worked, fine mold. Fine mold must then be worked and pressed in among the roots. . . .

No manure is to be placed in contact with the roots." I mix well-finished compost and leaf mold (see chapter 10) into the planting soil and work that around the roots. Manure is too strong a fertilizer. Be sure your compost/leaf-mold soil makes good contact with the roots. Unfilled air pockets can dry out roots.

Working in soil around tree roots

8. Olmsted had his men mound up soil around the trunk to hold it in place until the roots grew and anchored into the soil. Today, we secure the trunk to a stake with a soft tie of tree tape, rubber hose, or a band of old carpet. You want to prevent the trunk from rocking back and forth in the wind. Don't use a thin, hard material like wire to tie the trunk, because it will cut into and damage the outer cambium, its growing layer.

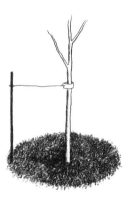

Staking tree

9. "No tree or shrub should be planted deeper than it has previously stood." [4]
10. He didn't say it, probably because he thought it was so obvious, but I'm sure he did it: Water the new plant well.

conditions. By 1889, however, Stanford was focusing all his energies on completing the campus buildings, and work on the arboretum came to a halt, never to be resumed.

In this century, irrigation has made it feasible to grow traditional turf lawns in the arid regions throughout the western United States, but water is still a limited resource in most of those areas, and the practice is wasteful. The genius that Olmsted followed is to this day more appropriate.

By the last decade of the century, Olmsted was at the height of his powers. He visited Europe again, and took his sons into business with him — John as the business manager and Frederick Jr. as a design apprentice. Within his lifetime, and largely due to his own prominence, landscape gardening had been raised in America from the status of menial labor to that of a profession and an art. Fred Jr. held the first Chair in Landscape Architecture at Harvard.

After Olmsted died in 1903, young Fred continued the business, working out of the family home and offices, known as Fairsted, until 1950. The corner lot at 99 Warren Street in Brookline, Massachusetts, is now a historic landmark. Its layout includes the miniature park that is the model American backyard, that quiet corner of nature in the city, with its shrubs, trees, and lawn.

Aunt Bumps

*I*f anyone ever led me down the garden path, it was Gertrude Jekyll. With the best intentions, of course. Gardening for her was high art, a cheerful absorption in the beauty of the natural world, and she liked nothing better than sharing it with others. When I first read Miss Jekyll's books, I knew I had found a friend.

Miss Jekyll (rhymes with *treacle*) was an avid gardener whose long life extended from the mid-1800s well into our own century. For over fifty of those years, she and her partner, the architect Edwin Lutyens, helped to set a style and define a period in English garden history, one that embodied the best of an age, one that came to an end, along with so much else, in World War I.

The Jekyll-Lutyens partnership was so aesthetically influential in its milieu that it came to symbolize the taste of a certain English class: the thing to own, if you were wealthy and cultured in the Edwardian era, was "a Lutyens house with a Jekyll garden."

Ironically, though, the Jekyll-Lutyens style drew its inspiration from the humblest classes of the day, from the simple elegance of such peasant craftsmen as the stone cutter, the plasterer, and the village thatcher. Remarked Miss Jekyll of her interest in these activities: "I could watch any clever workman for hours. Even the shoveling and shaping of ground is pleasant to see, but when it comes to a craftsman of long experience using the tool that seems to have become a part of himself, the attraction is so great that I can hardly tear myself away." [1]

And as often as not her involvement turned to more than just passive observation — she liked nothing more than taking an active hand in whatever manual endeavor was going on around her. After showing Gertrude around his Berkeley farm, a contemporary gentleman commented, "Good chap, Jekyll, knows how to feel a fat beast." [2] During construction of a new family home shortly after her father's death, Gertrude supervised the work, climbing up ladders to inspect roofing, drawing her hand along windowsills to feel their sanded texture. At one point she even started down a well to examine the newly exposed geological strata, but was dissuaded by the workmen, ostensibly due to their concern for her safety, but also no doubt because they feared having to haul her not-inconsiderable weight back to the surface.

The simplicity of Gertrude and Edwin's aesthetic roots showed itself in their use of native stone and hand-crafted construction, and their plantings of old-fashioned cottage-garden flowers — pinks, catmint, lilies, and the like. Extensive craft labor made their work expensive, and it was only their renown among the wealthy (caused largely by the coverage of their projects in the influential journal *Country Life*) that enabled them to realize their luxurious plans. And even among this affluent clientele, Lutyen's devotion to the best materials and to architecture for architecture's sake (Gertrude once accused him of indulging in "architectonic inutility") earned him a reputation for being dear. Miss Jekyll confesses in her writings that they argued over budgets more than once.

Gertrude Jekyll is best known for originating the herbaceous border. This is an array of choice garden flowers arranged in loose, sinuous drifts of subtle color harmonies, planted in a long, rectangular bed, usually backed by a high stone wall or deep green hedge. Properly composed, a border like this has the air of an impressionist painting come to life. The essence of it is the placement of color in harmonies rather than sharp contrasts, a planting in which the tints and hues move in graduated steps through a portion of the spectrum. One border in Miss Jekyll's own legendary garden, Munstead Wood, began with muted blues, grays, and somber green foliage at one end, worked its way through pale yellows and light pinks to brighter yellows and oranges, crested in red dahlias and cannas in the middle, then descended back down the scale to cool violets and lavenders at the far end.

Miss Jekyll began her life in art as a painter. The watercolorist Hercules Brabazon was her teacher, and J. M. W. Turner a major inspiration. But it was in horticulture that she earned her place in history, one that still exerts a strong influence on gardeners today. She wrote fourteen books on gardening, many of which are not only still in print but still in active use. From professional designers like Russell Page and John Brooks to the backyard putterer searching for just the right combination of gray-green leaf and silver-pink bloom, her spirit is still very much with us.

Well-traveled, well-to-do, and witty, she was *Miss* Jekyll throughout her life. Perhaps it was the fact that she was plain, or that she was quite heavy. Perhaps it was because she was a woman of forbidding mien, one who did not suf-

Herbaceous flower border

fer fools gladly. Probably it was all of these things, plus the fact that her monkish devotion to her art kept conventional preoccupations at a distance. At any rate, she never recorded the slightest regret in the matter — her diaries, writings, and biographies are devoid of comment on the topic of romance or marriage.

She could hardly have had better preparation for the kind of life she was to lead than that provided her as a child. From her earliest years, she was encouraged to think for herself and chart her own aesthetic course. Her family was wealthy, and she grew up surrounded by good music, classical art, and fine gardens. She knew early on that she was expected to cultivate her taste and develop her mind.

Gertrude Jekyll was born in London on November 29, 1843. When she was five, her family moved to a large country mansion, Bramley House, in southwest Surrey. Although it has since been invaded by London's roads and mortar, Surrey was at that time the quintessence of gentle English countryside, a land of wood, weald, and river, of winding country paths and ancient stone bridges across the rivers Wey and Mole, a place of red poppies blooming alongside wagon ruts, of sunsets glimpsed through copses of white-barked birch. It's not hard to understand how this land won her heart, and why she came to know in her fingertips its sandy soil.

Since she had four brothers, all closer to her in age than her one sister, it's also not hard to understand how Gertrude grew up as something of a tomboy, "delighting to go up trees, and play cricket, and take wasps' nests after dark, and do dreadful things with gunpowder." [3] She often joined her brothers in such escapades as commandeering a beer cooler and pressing it into service as a makeshift ferry to cross their millpond. When the boys went off to school, Gertrude

stayed home, as girls did then, but she continued to roam the country lanes alone, looking for adventure.

When she was nine, Gertrude decided to bring discipline to her previously haphazard acquaintance with the local wildflowers. With the help of a governess, she began to study a popular handbook of the day, *Flowers of the Field*, using the first of three copies she would wear out in her lifetime. She became quite the well-informed young botanist, familiar with the wayside wildlings as well as the more formal plantings around Bramley House.

She had also by this time commenced to draw and paint, and to spend hours observing the common folk at work. Standing by the doors and workbenches of village artisans, she became a familiar presence throughout the community. As the knife sharpener turned his stone, as the mason laid his brick and mortar, as the mower swung his scythe through the gleaming stalks, she was there, hearing the music of the wheel, the tap of the trowel, the swish of the blade, watching and sometimes taking part with her own hands, learning skills uncommon to a young lady of her station.

In 1861, Miss Jekyll enrolled in the Kensington School of Art in London — an endeavor almost as unorthodox for a Victorian girl as playing with gunpowder. With its bohemian overtones, art was hardly the conventional pursuit for young women of that day, but Gertrude didn't give this a second thought. At age eighteen, she knew she had talent, and she was right: her instructor at Kensington made use of her drawings when he prepared his lectures for publication.

In 1863, Miss Jekyll was invited by a friend from art school, Mary Newton, to accompany her and her husband on a trip to Greece and the Near East. Charles Newton, Keeper of the Greek and Roman Antiquities at the British Museum and a longtime acquaintance of the Jekyll family, had planned this trip to Rhodes and Constantinople to research a book on classical archeology. The prospect of joining the Newtons for a few months, sketching the Mediterranean and breathing the air of classical times, appealed to Gertrude.

On their journey, Miss Jekyll and Mrs. Newton sketched constantly. One of Mrs. Newton's portraits shows Miss Jekyll in long, full skirt, carrying an easel, folding chair, and bags of supplies, with water bottle secured to her waist, marching through crowds to the next "view." In another drawing, Gertrude is shown at work, seated on her folding chair, painting one group of Turkish natives while another group, just as large, stands attentively behind her, peering over her shoulder. Her diary from the period is full of detailed descriptions, no doubt intended to provide reminders for later paintings: "Nov. 3 — We paid a visit to a native family. Their faces are much painted, the eyebrows painted to meet between the eyes, and their nails and finger tips stained red with henna. . . . We asked if they would sit for us in our garden."[4] Rocky coastlines, the scenery of the Dardanelles and the Bosphorus, places, buildings, and people — including the beautiful bodies of men she saw passing in the streets — all were recorded as part of her visual memories.

Even her shopping lists reveal Miss Jekyll's visual preoccupation. One day, her diary tells us, she "bought some Stambul handkerchiefs of beautiful colors, some Turkish knives, and blue glass camel-beads, a red waistband, and a pair of yellow shoes."[5] On a subsequent tour of Italy some thirteen years later, these artistic inclinations persisted. As always, she had her eye out for beautiful handiwork and was ready to pounce whenever she found it: in Venice a relative found her triumphantly stealing away from a "sacristy laden with vestments 'hot from the priest's back' and yards of lace ripped off with her own hands — a little transaction more easily to be effected in those happy far-off days than now."[6]

And of course she made detailed observations about the Near Eastern flora: cyclamen, narcissus, crocus, iris, and maidenhair ferns — plants that she encountered growing wild. It was on this trip that she first befriended the herbs and other gray-leaved plants that were to become such a distinctive element in her gardens. Many — bay, rosemary, thyme, cistus — are aromatic, and when she brushed against them in later years she was often reminded of this trip.

It is due in part to Miss Jekyll that these plants have come to play the role that they so often do in contemporary garden schemes. Their silvery values serve well as both foil and unifying theme in garden design, furnishing a consistently soothing tone as the more intensely colored flowers come

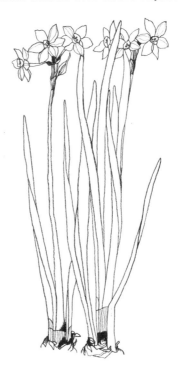

Narcissus

and go throughout the year. Their fragrances are welcome and their rugged and unusual textures offer a pleasant contrast to many cultivated plants. Moreover, they are durable: matted thyme, veronica, and chamomile can be walked on without much harm. In a cultured garden scene, they lend a refreshing note of wild vigor. Almost without exception, herbs are easy to grow, and some — artemisia, sage, and rue, for instance — have found great favor in companion planting, helping ward off pests and disease.

As well as having an eye for their beauty, Miss Jekyll also had the gardener's appreciation for the relationship of these plants to their climate and terrain. The aromatic herbs she met grow in dry ground, under a hot sun, exposed to wind and sea air, unsheltered by trees. In such conditions, their silvery-gray foliage is an adaptive device for reflecting intense sunlight. In addition, these leaves often are covered with small hairs that create a microclimate, helping to provide shade at the leaf surface.

Bulbs, rhizomes, and corms of the Mediterranean region solve the exposure problem in a different way, by storing moisture and nutrients in their swollen underground stems. When spring comes these plants hasten into bloom and send up new leaves to quickly photosynthesize replacements for their depleted supplies, then just as quickly go dormant again by the time the full heat of summer has returned. The maidenhair fern is the exception, nature's way of breaking her own rules. Otherwise defenseless, it must seek refuge from the sun in the most rudimentary of ways, by growing only in the cool shade of moist, rocky outcroppings. All of these plants intrigued Miss Jekyll, and she collected samples of many of them, along with the seeds of a Turkish date and a wild solanum. It seems they did well for her back home under cloudy English skies.

When Miss Jekyll returned from her Mediterranean trip on the day after Christmas, 1863, she was just twenty years old. The next decade was a period of active socializing and intense artistic pursuit for her. Her interests steadily expanded to include gilding, embroidery, and other media. Under the encouragement of two special friends, Jacques and Leonie Blumenthal, her talent for interior decoration matured. From Bramley she made frequent outings to London, and every year she went abroad, to the Blumenthal chalet above Lake Geneva, to Italy to study gilding and carving, or to Paris to take voice lessons.

In her wide circle of friends, Miss Jekyll came to be

known for the unsurpassable quality of her work — draperies, gildings, carvings, and cushions embroidered with dandelions, mistletoe, strawberries, or pomegranates. It was all avidly sought after, at first by those who knew her, later by private collectors and museums.

In 1868, the Jekylls moved to a new home at Wargrave, on the Thames. The change was her father's idea, and Gertrude was an obedient daughter, but she was distinctly unhappy at being uprooted from her beloved Surrey countryside. Fortunately, the new house at Wargrave provided ample opportunities for exercising her artistic talents to the fullest, creating "Chinese screens, pear-wood frames, imitation Rhodian pots, open-work silver pins, gold stands for China," and much more.[7]

Steadily, gardening began to claim more of her attention. Opium poppies and the white *Lychnis viscosa* (now known as *Viscaria vulgaris "alba"*) were added to the grounds at Wargrave. Visiting nurseries and roaming the countryside in search of collectible native plants began to take the place of jaunts to London. Even in these earliest efforts, it was already clear that Gertrude's garden designs constituted a radical departure from the predominant practice of the day, the "bedding-out" fashion that placed great emphasis on geometrical massing of bold, bright, contrasting colors — yellow calceolaria, red sage, and blue lobelia, for example. Miss Jekyll was headed in a more naturalistic direction, one that focused on the blending of subtle color gradations in loose, organic groupings, and one that paid special attention to the planting of wild herbs and common, cottage-garden flowers.

In 1876, Gertrude's father died suddenly. Her mother decided to leave Wargrave and return to Surrey. Purchasing some twenty acres on Munstead heath, she had a house built. By 1878, mother, daughter, and the two boys still at home were firmly ensconced in the new residence.

This is where Gertrude designed and created her first garden. It began with a terrace of native stone, lined with handsome tubs and pots for added foliage and color. Then a lawn went in, bordered by hedges and flowering shrubs. Naturalized bulbs pointed the way from cultivated to wilder, woodier areas. Despite her sorrow at the reason for the move, Gertrude was delighted to be back in Surrey.

Throughout the 1880s, the iconoclastic William Robinson who, like Gertrude, championed the use of cottage-garden flowers, was a frequent visitor. Her own reputation as a fine gardener was spreading. In 1881 she was invited to judge at the Botanic Show, predecessor of today's world-renowned Chelsea Flower Show. She befriended neighbor G. F. Wilson, whose property was later bequeathed to the Royal Horticultural Society. Visitors, both gardeners and painters, dropped by to pay their respects to her living compositions of color and light.

At some point in that same decade, Miss Jekyll purchased her own triangular piece of property, some fifteen acres or so, located directly across the road from her mother's house. Appropriately enough, the first thing she did was to begin developing the grounds of her new estate, known henceforth as Munstead Wood. (The house, it seems, could wait.)

It was at about this time that Miss Jekyll obtained her first formal gardening client, about whom nothing more is known than his name: a Mr. Okell of Manchester. She had been giving away advice for years, on one occasion even replying to a newspaper ad, sending a plan and seedlings to a factory worker who wanted to make a window box. That she answered at all shows something of her generosity of spirit in sharing her delight in gardening. It also represents something of a minor landmark in gardening annals, because what she sent were the makings of a small rock garden — saxifrage, squills, and a few rocks — and this was at the very beginning of the rock-gardening movement.

By 1891, her fate was sealed. Now almost fifty, Miss Jekyll had been growing steadily more nearsighted for years, a condition made worse by the demanding detail of most of the media she worked in. At last her eyesight became so poor she consulted a well-known German ophthalmologist. His discouraging prognosis meant that she would be forced to give up many of her pursuits — embroidery and painting in particular. Though this was a blow, it brought her closer to becoming a full-time gardener, for there was a canvas so large she could happily continue working on it no matter how myopic she might get.

A year passed. Although she had been planting steadily at Munstead Wood for some time now, she still had no house there. The time had come to build. Letters were sent to colleagues, seeking advice. Ruskin recommended the use of thick oaken timbers and white plaster walls. Then one day in May 1892, while taking tea with neighbor Harry Mangles, Gertrude made the acquaintance of another guest, a shy but irreverent young man who, as luck would have it, was a promising local architect. (In fact, there is some hint that Miss Jekyll contrived the meeting, with the cooperation of Mr. Mangles.) His name was Edwin Lutyens (pronounced "Lutchins"), and he had been raised in nearby Farnham. Like Miss Jekyll, he had passed much of his childhood roaming the Surrey countryside. Going off to school, moreover, had been denied young Edwin too, because he had contracted rheumatic fever and been under standing orders not to strain his weakened heart. At age twenty, having apprenticed in the office of a nearby architect, he hung out his shingle and began developing a practice.

Miss Jekyll and young Lutyens hardly exchanged a word that day. Only when she was actually stepping into her ponycart for the ride home did she turn to him and announce that she would be pleased to entertain him at tea the following Saturday. Issued by a person of Miss Jekyll's standing, this was more of a summons than an invitation, but Lutyens was well aware of the potential benefits of an association with her and was only too happy to oblige.

What transpired that following Saturday and at their many subsequent meetings was more a marriage of minds than the usual client-consultant relationship. Soon they were referring to one another as "Ned" and "Aunt Bumps," and taking rides in the ponycart to survey the local crafts that she wished to employ in the creation of her home. (Miss Jekyll objected now and then to his jests about her "innocent rotundities," but Ned was irrepressible — soon he was referring to the estate as "Bumpstead Wood.")

Lutyens shared Miss Jekyll's admiration for the honest elegance of the English rural arts, and she loved his wit, objections notwithstanding. His puns, sketches, and doodles won her affection as surely as any Surrey wildflower could, and she had the pleasure of helping bring to maturity his keen eye for architecture.

Soon they were meeting almost daily. Ned would drop by in the afternoon, and he and Bumps would climb up into the ponycart to make their rounds. (She had seen to it that the rein guide was mounted slightly off-center to give her extra room on the seat.) Her severe myopia made their trips a hazy dream for her, a harrowing series of near-misses for him. But somehow, while he might be staring anxiously at looming stone walls and solid oaks along the way, she was always able to see flowers well enough to spy out the tiniest roadside treasure.

Their first collaboration was a small house, later known as The Hut. Completed in 1894, it was probably conceived of as a workshop and cottage retreat for occasional use while Gertrude was still officially in residence with her mother. The following year, however, Mrs. Jekyll died and Gertrude's brother Herbert inherited the house. Gertrude moved into The Hut while she and Ned undertook the job of designing and constructing the main house at Munstead Wood.

Building was under way by the summer of 1896. The grounds, which had been evolving for nearly a decade by then, were well in hand. The vegetable garden was well dug and manured. A nut walk had been cleared and planted. Although Miss Jekyll was able to support a work force of eleven gardeners, she did much of the work herself.

The house, when it was finished, was more of a distinguished hermitage than anything else, in which everything was quiet and subdued, with cozy entrance halls, neat sitting rooms, wide stone hearths, broad, low beams, and solid staircases. In 1897, Miss Jekyll moved in. It was a home she would occupy for over thirty years, sharing it only with a multitude of cats and a vast collection of textiles, ceramics, glassware, stains, samples, swatches, paints, brushes, pencils, and more, all neatly catalogued and stowed away in drawers, cabinets, and shelves. Lutyens took no commission for his work on Bumpstead Wood.

(Those cats, incidentally, were very dear to Miss Jekyll. A relative recalls that trying to find a place to sit in her house was like playing a hopeless game of musical chairs, one in which Tattle Bat and Pinkie Boy and their many companions had already staked a claim to every seat. Miss Jekyll, reports another visitor, attached a length of string to the back of her own favorite chair so that she could entertain herself and the cats by surreptitiously giving it a tug now and then, reaching behind her as though to scratch her neck, when receiving a less than scintillating guest.)

In the midst of all this activity, Miss Jekyll was also writing prolifically on gardening, and her writing was widely read. The *Edinburgh Review* brought out an article on the history of gardening by her. *The Guardian* published a series of her gardening guides, which were then collected and revised into her first book, *Wood and Garden*. A month-by-month chronicle of gardening, *Wood and Garden* also points up the value of keeping an ongoing record of procedures and plans that the gardener can look over in preparing for the next year. Miss Jekyll makes it clear in this book that she fully sympathizes with the trepidation felt by most novices when they begin:

Many people who love flowers and wish to do some practical gardening are at their wit's end to know what to do and how to begin. Like a person who is on skates for the first time, they feel that, what with the bright steel runners, and the slippery surfaces, and the sense of helplessness, there are more ways to tumbling about than of progressing safely in any one direction. And in gardening the beginner must feel this kind of perplexity and helplessness, and indeed there is a great deal to learn, only it is pleasant instead of perilous, and the many tumbles by the way only teach and do not hurt.[8]

The instant popularity of *Wood and Garden* prompted more. Articles in *Country Life* were expanded into *Lilies for English Gardens*, *Wall and Water Gardens*, and *Roses for English Gardens*, all published in the earliest years of this century, all

illustrated with photographs taken by the author herself —
another of her avocations.

Of course, during this entire period Miss Jekyll also had a
large garden to manage, one that had become a showcase
for the new naturalistic style, and one that led to a flood of
commissions for garden designs. The first decade of the
twentieth century was a period of peak creative activity for
the Jekyll-Lutyens collaboration. Nearly sixty houses were
designed in this period, a list that includes such evocative
names as The Orchards, Tigbourne Court, Grey Walls,
Folly Farm, Little Thakeham, Lindisfarne Castle, Hester-
combe, Barton St. Mary, and Great Mayham. Now and
then, in her long career, Miss Jekyll did have occasion to
work with other architects; however, in comparison with
Ned they were, as she once commented, like suet to quick-
silver.

The publisher of *Country Life*, Edward Hudson, became
such a proponent of the Jekyll-Lutyens style that he commissioned Lutyens to design the magazine's London offices,
the architect's first urban project. (Having chosen to use
Christopher Wren's Hampton Court as his model, Lutyens
characteristically began to refer to the job as being done in a
"Wrenaissance" style.)

For many of us today, the most pertinent example of their
work is Millmead, one of the few places where Miss Jekyll
worked on a backyard scale. Millmead is doubly intriguing
in this respect because it was not a commissioned project:
she bought the property and created its garden purely for
the joy of it, as well as to make something of a monument to
the happiness of her childhood at Bramley, which the Millmead site happened to overlook.

Millmead is approximately one-half acre in size, about 75
by 350 feet. The entrance, like that at Munstead Wood, is

quiet and green, soothing but unremarkable. Forecourt plantings of bergenia, clematis, and box offer a hint of more to come, through the garden gate to the right of the house.

One common response to a site like Millmead is to follow the Olmsted approach, hiding the lot's rectangularity with soft, wavy bunches of trees and shrubs, masses of leafy foliage. Commendable as it often is, this strategy can lead to wasted space when applied to a small place.

Miss Jekyll chose a different treatment. Working with Lutyens, she gave the property an unapologetically geometrical feel, one that capitalizes on and does not try to hide its basic form. The back garden, which constitutes over half the total area of the site, is divided into four main levels, something like outdoor rooms, separated from one another by both thick plantings and slight changes in elevation marked by short flights of steps.

The first and highest area, the one closest to the house, is a rose garden, underplanted with lavender and catnip. Surrounding the roses are snowballs, forsythia, and lilacs, with daylilies and numerous other perennials — all meant to lend a note of leafy luxuriance, but to do so with restrained color so as not to distract from the focal point, the roses in the center.

From the first level, the visitor moves down to the second

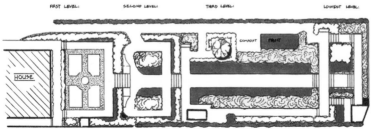

Millmead

one, defined primarily by two long beds filled with perennial flowers and shrubs running parallel to the central path. Stepping down another short flight of broad sandstone stairs brings the visitor to the third level, one characterized by a large pear tree and a screen of shrubs hiding the compost pile and work area. On the other side of the path is another perennial flower border, this one dedicated to summer blossoms.

Down a few more steps, this time curving around a stone wall, and the visitor has arrived in the last and lowest section of the garden. Here a garden seat invites one's attention to move from admiration of the low, delicate epimediums, campanula, saxifrage, and aubretia to the vista out over the surrounding countryside. The view is a fine example of the technique of borrowing or "appropriating" neighboring attractions, one pioneered in England and made much use of by Olmsted and other landscape gardeners.

We see in Millmead that Miss Jekyll shared the fundamental respect of many of her predecessors for the genius of the place. "In the arrangement of any site," she noted, "the natural conditions of the place should first be studied." [9] What Millmead also demonstrates, however, is Miss Jekyll's constant and primary interest in the cottage garden. All of her work on larger estates, no matter what size, was simply an expansion of this original source of inspiration. When Millmead was completed, she rented it out, taking care to choose tenants who would appreciate her work. It remains a private home to this day.

In the first decade of the twentieth century, Miss Jekyll was in her sixties and at the height of her fame. But the shadows were lengthening. William Morris died in 1896, Dean Reynolds Hole in 1904, Hercules Brabazon two years later. Feeling her age more and more, she tended to stay at home. Although she would live almost three more decades, Miss Jekyll made the last visit of her life to London in 1904.

However, she continued to work as hard as ever at her writing and her design work, and on maintaining the garden masterpiece that was Munstead Wood. As her journals indicate, her day was carefully scheduled:

8:00 A.M.	Called [by her maid, Florence Hayter]
9–9:30	Breakfast, a substantial meal
9:30–11	Letters and garden orders. Workroom.
11	A cup of soup. Till 1 P.M. in the garden or workroom, according to weather.
1–1:30	Lunch
1:30–2	Read the newspapers
2–3	Rest in bedroom
3–4:30	In garden or workroom, according to weather
4:30	Tea
5–7:30	Garden in summer if fine, workroom in winter
7:30–8	Dinner
8–10:30 or 11	Reading and listening in bed [i.e., to the radio][10]

A special project was the continuing development of the Munstead strain of the polyanthus primrose. The result of a natural cross between the primrose (*Primula vulgaris*) and the cowslip (*Primula veris*), this flower has been selected and bred for centuries. In Miss Jekyll's hands it took on new highlights of white and yellow, and is still available from specialists, such as Far North Gardens (see appendix A).

World War I brought a grand era in gardening to an end forever. During the war, Miss Jekyll reduced her staff and converted more of the grounds at Munstead to vegetable gardens to help feed her neighbors. At the end of the war, the Imperial War Graves Commission asked her to help design plantings for the millions of British men buried overseas.

Things were never the same. Villagers uprooted from the old ways and thrown into close contact with their "betters" in the fear and squalor of the trenches were not likely to return unchanged to the past order, at the same low wages. Few who left as gardeners returned as gardeners. Estates grew more expensive to make and maintain. Miss Jekyll herself sounded the knell of the passing age when she complained that "the cost of labor is ruinous — and everything else." [11]

Today, most of the gardens created by Aunt Bumps and Ned are either gone altogether or in disrepair, including Munstead Wood. A few are maintained by England's National Trust, and some are in private hands, kept up by individuals out of sheer love of a lost age of gardening style.

As the years passed, Miss Jekyll retreated ever more firmly into the security of Munstead Wood, resisting the encroachments of the modern world. She would not use a typewriter. Until she had experienced its companionability on a cold winter's evening, she objected to the radio that her brother had given her. Her reputation continued to grow, however, and she was obliged to turn away a steady stream of requests for invitations to view Munstead. Christmas always brought a deluge of cards, prompting wry outbursts like this: "Forgive us our Christmases as we forgive them that Christmas against us." [12]

When she began to have trouble walking, Ned obtained a wheelchair for her, and she patrolled the garden in it, gathering seed from her most cherished specimens, particularly the giant *Erythronium* and the new blue poppy. In 1932 there were enough rose petals to make 11,000 potpourri, a job that took a mob of Jekylls four days to complete.

Her brother Herbert, her last link with the past, died in

Miss Jekyll

September 1932. Miss Jekyll followed three months later, on December 8. She left behind almost nine decades of fine work, a new style that gardeners everywhere admire and emulate, and an enormous collection of treasures, scrupulously catalogued, filling every nook and cranny of the house at Bumpstead Wood.

SEVEN

St. Wilfred

*G*ardening is not solely an artistic pursuit. Nature has always had healing properties for man as well, both literally and in a more ineffable sense. Nowhere is this more evident than in the long tradition of herb culture, and in the story of a man who forged a critical link between classical and Christian views of the garden, one who was himself a devoted cultivator of herbs, the medieval monk Walafried Strabo.

Walafried, or Wilfred, was born over 1,000 years before Miss Jekyll and Frederick Olmsted, in 809, in what is now southwestern Germany. At that time, this region was part of the empire of one of the greatest of all Frankish kings, Charlemagne, who ruled both the secular army and the religious state. Wilfred was born in humble circumstances, of illiterate peasant folk, in a village of small, one-room cottages with thatched roofs and walls made of mud and straw. The life was agricultural and the agriculture was elementary.

Near each dwelling was a well-manured kitchen garden, devoted mainly to cabbage and turnips. Because metal was scarce, the earth was broken with rude wooden spades and other implements. The cabbage and turnips, plus peas and beans and a bit of semiwild pork now and then, were only occasional variations: cereals, grown on lightly cultivated common lands outside the village proper, were the staples of the village diet. Baked into bread, cooked into a heavy stew, or even fermented into a thick beer, barley, oats, and such constituted the daily fare.

Wilfred was born with a squint — thus the epithet *strabo*, from the Greek word meaning "twisted." This may have been the reason why his parents, perhaps regarding him as marked by God or unfit for the demanding life of the village, took him when he was eight years old to the nearby monastery of Augia, now called Reichenau, an island in Lake Constance. There he was left, a *puerus oblatus* (literally, "offered boy"), to be raised by the brothers of the Benedictine order that had built Augia there a century or so earlier. Wilfred took to monastic life without recorded regret at being separated from his family. He did well, made friends, rose to a position of power and influence, and forever after referred to the monastery as his home, as *Augia felix*, or "happy Augia."

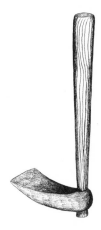

Reichenau

As well as being seats of learning and repositories of the intellectual heritage of the classical age, medieval monasteries were also responsible for training the administrators of the realm, including Charlemagne's successors. Though Charlemagne himself had died when Wilfred was quite young, his kingdom had passed into the hands of one of his sons, Louis the Pious, and the Benedictine practice of service to the crown was still very much the custom as Wilfred grew into young manhood.

One of the more important traditions that the medieval era inherited from classical authors was that of herbs and herbals. Herbs are, of course, simply wild plants that man has found a use for, as medicines, seasonings, or perfumes. Many are also quite decorative. Traditional herbal folklore was as widely practiced in ninth-century Europe as it had been in ancient Greece, or as it is to this day in much of the Third World. By virtue of their central role in the preservation of classical knowledge, including the great herbals of Greek and Roman authors, medieval monasteries acquired special authority over the arts of healing in the Middle Ages.

The fact that much of their knowledge of herbs was drawn from pre-Christian sources posed something of a theological dilemma for these clerical herbalists. To be sure, herbs had long been regarded as being of divine origin and were the object of much classical mythologizing. *Artemisia*, for example, a silvery-leaved genus that includes sagebrush, wormwood, and tarragon, is named after Artemis (or Diana), goddess of the forest, wild plants, and the moon. Another Greek demigod, Chiron the Centaur, taught Achilles that yarrow leaves could be used to stanch the flow of blood, a bit of information the warrior put to use in treating his fallen comrades at Troy, and which is now memorialized in yarrow's botanical name, *Achillea millefolium*.

To the medieval Christian herbalist reading a classical work like Dioscorides' *De Materia Medica*, all this was a bit troubling. Inclined though he was to sympathize with the view that everything in nature had a divine purpose, he was also taught to regard Greek and Roman views on such matters as pagan, misguided, and even sacrilegious. Following them uncritically might jeopardize his own prospects for eternity. Thus the medieval attitude toward classical herb culture faced a fundamental dilemma. Its failure to resolve this conflict led to neglect of the foundations of descriptive botany laid by men like Theophrastus. Wilfred's deceptively humble reaffirmation of the inherent Christian goodness of nature is an early and rare effort to reunite man with his classical legacy.

Growing up in Augia, reading authors like Dioscorides not only to gain pharmaceutical knowledge but also to improve his command of classical tongues, Wilfred was to become first a student of the tradition of herb culture and then a contributor to it. His garden poem, *The Hortulus,* is an invaluable bridge from the sacred order of his day to our own secular, skeptical age. In making his garden and his poem, Wilfred was curiously transformed in a way that allowed him to reach beyond his own sectarian environment to a point where both the Garden of Eden and the ancient Greek *paradeisos* (an enclosed park with shade trees, sparkling streams, and ripe fruit hanging ready to pluck) became one and the same.

Wilfred quickly became one of Augia's star pupils. By the time he was in his teens, it was clear to Father Grimald, master of the school at Augia, that he had a gift for languages, particularly for the suspiciously pagan art of Latin verse. So fluent, in fact, was Wilfred that he was soon assigned demanding compositional chores, ranging from messages to abbots of neighboring monasteries to recording the deathbed visions of a fellow monk, visions that were politically sensitive because they depicted Charlemagne himself in limbo. Despite occasional fears on the part of his elders that his familiarity with the works of such profane humanists as Cicero might contaminate his thinking, Wilfred not only fulfilled his writing assignments with skill, but soon exceeded the capabilities of Augia's teaching staff. At the age of seventeen he was sent north to the monastery at Fulda to study under the most renowned teacher of the age, Hrabanus Maurus, himself the author of the *Physica,* an herbal that Wilfred undoubtedly came to know well.

Under Maurus's tutelage, Wilfred continued to distinguish himself, and by the age of twenty was again promoted, this time to the royal court at Aachen, to teach Louis the Pious's fourth son, Charles, then just six years of age. For the next decade, Wilfred remained at Aachen, becoming known and trusted by the royal circle in ways that would continue to involve him in politics for the rest of his life and that would ultimately cause his death.

When Wilfred eventually took his leave of Aachen, in 838, he was almost thirty. He headed, of course, for home, *Augia felix*, but not without recognition for his long years of service to the crown: this time when the "young barbarian" (as Wilfred was fond of describing himself in his youth) passed through the monastery's gates, it was King Louis's pleasure that he did so as its abbot.

Wilfred's respite was short-lived. Two years later Louis died and the disputes over his successor that broke out threw the kingdom into a turmoil. Augia and the lands around it came under the rule of a royal brother — Louis the German — who was hostile to the Benedictine order and whose men-at-arms drove Wilfred out of Augia so hastily that, as he wrote Maurus, he was forced to leave his sandals behind and flee barefoot.

Two more years were to pass before Wilfred was able to return home safely. And it was at this point that his life took its most significant turn. Weary of the violence around him, disillusioned by the suffering that pious men were so willing to inflict on one another, Wilfred turned to the source of solace whose image is found at the heart of his religion: the garden. Within the walls of Augia, Wilfred was to recreate a simple paradise and, as he did, to immortalize his work in elegant Latin verse in *The Hortulus* (the Little Garden).

In its reference to Paestrum, a city renowned in antiquity for its twice-blooming roses, *The Hortulus* opens with a nod to Virgil's *Georgics*. As so many gardens are, Wilfred's was first conceived in the earliest days of spring. The air was freshening, the sky clear and bright. Warm southerly winds were beginning to blow again. Winter had retreated from the hills and valleys around Augia, and nature's resurrection was once more touching the bare branches and brown earth with green.

Outside the door of Wilfred's cell was a courtyard, the ideal place, he thought, for an herb garden. Facing east, it would catch the early light and warmth of the rising sun. Surrounded by high walls, there would, to be sure, be places in the shade that wouldn't get enough light. Others would tend to stay too dry because overhanging eaves would deflect the water from the spring rains. On the whole, however, the place was promising, and Wilfred set to with a will.

After careful observation of the garden site, the first step, he noted, was to improve the soil. His feelings on this step, epitomizing as they do the experience of every gardener, are worth quoting directly:

For whatever the land you possess, whether it be where sand
And gravel lie barren and dead, or where fruits grow heavy
In rich moist ground; whether high on a steep hillside,
Easy ground in the plain or rough among sloping valleys —
Wherever it is, your land cannot fail to produce
Its native plants. If you do not let laziness clog
Your labor, if you do not insult with misguided efforts
The gardener's multifarious wealth, and if you do not
Refuse to harden or dirty your hands in the open air
Or to spread whole baskets of dung on the sun-parched soil —
Then, you may rest assured, your soil will not fail you.[1]

Long neglected, the little space in front of Wilfred's door was covered with a thick tangle of nettles and weeds. Taking his wooden mattock in hand, he went to work, clearing them away, loosening the earth to allow air and moisture in. The soil was better than he thought, he soon learned, for as he started to dig he saw earthworms, a welcome indicator of life. He also discovered mole tunnels, which he carefully filled in, wondering as he did if he might be forced to resort to sterner measures to discourage the moles, such as the herbal poisons aconite and black hellebore. As he pondered the problem, Virgil's remarks on the "moles deprived of sight" no doubt came to mind (*Georgics*, Book I, lines 181–183).

With the aid of some of the newest *oblati*, Wilfred next formed raised rectangular beds, placing wooden planks on end to form boxes, which he then filled with loose soil. This was the typical way to make an herb garden in the Middle Ages and is still a perfectly sound method for giving herbs the good drainage they enjoy.

Setting down his mattock, Wilfred next took up a rake and carefully worked the top few inches of earth in each bed into a good "tilth," a fine surface free of clods and stones, suitable for sowing seed.

Finally, some days later, it was time to plant. From stores of seed harvested from previous years' gardens, as well as from pieces of plants dug up elsewhere on Augia's grounds, the beds were planted. Water was brought in ceramic jugs and dribbled onto the surface of each bed gently, so as not to wash away the seed or disturb the delicate young shoots.

Now Wilfred began to squint at the skies, watching for the clouds that would herald the arrival of "heaven's benison," the spring rains that were so crucial to the viability of each new plant. Arrive they did, and soon the beds were covered with a fine carpet of green. Even a few of the mature plants that Wilfred had taken up bodily and moved "more dead than alive" from elsewhere on the grounds flourished in their new location, reveling in the pleasure of newly turned soil. As the plants grew, Wilfred turned his attention in *The Hortulus* to the special features of each one.

First came sage, or salvia, from the same etymological root as *salvation*. As Wilfred observed, sage must be pruned back regularly or it will shade out its own inner branches and grow stemmy and brown in the middle. A favorite in any medieval garden, sage was used for so wide a variety of purposes, both culinary and medicinal, that the attitude of the age has been described as, "Why should a man die while sage grows in his garden?" [2]

Next came rue, fragrant and bitter, a poisonous emetic that was homeopathically used as an antidote for poisoning. Wilfred undoubtedly remembered the advice of the herbalist Pseudo-Apuleius, who recommended washing the forehead with rue as a remedy for forgetfulness.

Rue was followed by southernwood, good for treating fevers and gout, an ailment that had afflicted Charlemagne in his later years. And in their turn, wormwood, horehound, fennel, iris, lovage, chervil, poppy, clary, mint, pennyroyal, celery, betony, agrimony, tansy, catnip, and radish were all

Sage, *Salvia officinalis*

described, with brief notes on their beneficial properties. Of these plants, all except three — wormwood, tansy, and horehound — were also included in lists developed under Charlemagne's rule that mandated what every town in his realm would grow. Although Wilfred's garden was not created in response to any external decree, his choice of plants was probably intended in part to express his devotion to Charlemagne and his successors.

The Hortulus ended, as it must, with elegies on the two plants of greatest symbolic meaning for medieval Christians, the lily and the rose, standing for the power of faith and the blood of the martyrs.

Wilfred, it should be added, also grew a plant or two for purely gustatory appeal. One of these, the squash, caused him to anticipate in The Hortulus seeing "fruit handed round among the good things of the dinner table/And soaking up the rich fat in a piping dish." [3] And what's more, he added, if they are left on the vine until their skin is thoroughly hardened, squash make great wine vessels.

Melons were also to be found in a sunny patch at the foot of Wilfred's garden. Their big round shapes reminded him, he wrote, of nuts, eggs, or soap bubbles. Once fully ripened, they too were set before the brothers at Augia's table. In sank the knife, out flowed the cool juices, and then they were quickly broken into chunks whose "freshness and savor delight the palate." Moreover, this treat could be enjoyed by everyone, even the older monks, whose teeth were not always in the best of shape.

The Hortulus was dedicated to Wilfred's old teacher, Father Grimald. The scene Wilfred painted here is one of simple, sacred fraternity: Grimald is seated in a garden, surrounded by peach and apple trees — the trees of knowledge — as well as a new crop of students. Now and then a

fruit is pulled from the branches hanging heavy all about. The promise, in Wilfred's eyes, is the one that lay at the heart of his religion: for Grimald he wished the "palm that is green forever," eternal life.

For Wilfred, as for Virgil, the garden was both ordinary and holy. Despite its intimations of Eden, it was also a real and very human place, one whose yield, miraculous though it may be, was won by the sweat of a person's brow. The plants themselves, particularly the herbs, represent a healing presence that is ultimately divine. Like Christ the healer, the garden in Wilfred's view has the power to make men whole again.

Pleased as he was to be cultivating his hortulus, this was only another brief interlude in Wilfred's turbulent life. In 849, civil war was again raging, and Wilfred was once more called to serve the crown — this time to carry an important message between two combatants. Honorable man that he was, he left his happy Augia, never to return. On August 18, while fording the Loire, he slipped and drowned.

Now a popular tourist retreat, Reichenau is still a beautiful garden island, replete with grapes, greenhouses, and a flowered cloister.

EIGHT

This Too Could Be Yours

*A*lan Chadwick was born on July 27, 1909, in the fashionable seaside resort of St. Leonard's-on-Sea in southern England. The society that Chadwick grew up in was a paradoxical mixture of two worlds: village and empire. On the one hand, it was still very much the timeless, rural England of Miss Jekyll's artisans and their cottage gardens. On the other, it was also the world of colonial imperialism, a world in which the sun never set on the Union Jack.

Alan's aristocratic family lived on a country estate with one foot in both these worlds. Alan discovered gardening as a boy, first simply by watching the working gardeners his father employed, and second by visiting the great gardens of Britain and Europe.

Although Alan's father, Harry Chadwick, had trained as a barrister at Oxford, he never practiced the law. Instead, he sold two inherited estates, Puddleston Court in Hereford and Yarna Wood in Devon, shortly before Alan's birth and devoted himself to sports, particularly horse racing and rowing. In fact, it was at the rowing competitions held at Henley-on-Thames that Harry Chadwick first met his future wife, Elizabeth Alcock, who would become Alan's mother. The marriage, in 1907, was the second for both Harry and Elizabeth, and so Alan was born into a family of older half brothers and sisters, as well as one elder full brother, Seddon.

Before meeting Harry, Elizabeth had been the proprietress of an elegant Italian restaurant in London's West End, known for its lively bohemian atmosphere and frequented by actors, actresses, and members of society. Elizabeth was an accomplished painter and pianist and was also active in the Theosophical Society, where she made the acquaintance of, among others, Lady Emily Lutyens, Edwin's wife. Alan was, in Seddon's words, "a great favorite of his mother," and she clearly represented for him the artistic and spiritual side of life. Both parents were bilingual, Elizabeth in German and Harry in French.

Until he was about nine years old, Alan's family lived at Fawley, a ten-acre country estate in Sussex, near Eastbourne. Located in Hampden Park, Fawley must have been the picture of turn-of-the-century English manor life. The three-story brick and tile house, with billiard room, large main hall, and drawing room, was manned by a staff of five: a butler, a cook, two maids, and one other "inside" person. The large grounds, maintained by two gardeners who lived in a separate cottage, included a fair-sized kitchen garden, greenhouses, and a small lake with a boat. (A good idea of what life on such an estate was like can be obtained from reading Elizabeth Yandell's *Henry,* included in the Reading Guide at the end of this book.) The Chadwicks moved in influential circles: Harry went shooting with his neighbor, Lord Willingdon, who was to become Viceroy to India in 1931. A great uncle, Richard Seddon, was liberal Prime Minister of New Zealand in the early years of this century.

Due largely to his mother's influence, Alan was raised as a vegetarian and a pacifist, in an environment alive with occult speculation. When a schism developed in the Theosophical Society, Elizabeth Chadwick followed those who adhered to the teachings of Rudolf Steiner, founder of the new Anthroposophical Movement. Steiner, a magnetic personality himself, developed a spiritual philosophy based in part on his study of Goethe. He lectured widely on topics ranging from education to architecture to medicine, as well as farming. The latter lectures, given to a group of farmers at the Koberwitz estate near Basel, Switzerland, in 1924, form the basis of the biodynamic approach to gardening and farming, which is still thriving today. Alan first met the philosopher during Steiner's speaking tours in London in the early 1920s and was deeply impressed by the man.

Alan and Seddon attended a number of preparatory schools, in both England and Switzerland. Since their parents were fond of traveling on the Continent, the boys' education was a bit erratic, but this had its compensations: both became trilingual, in French, German, and English.

From an early age, Alan was interested in flower painting, and his art instructor at Fox and Russell's Academy in Vevey, Switzerland, tutored him in watercolor and in painting flower miniatures. One of Alan's favorite flower portraitists was the French artist Ignace M. J. T. Fantin-Latour.

During these same peripatetic years, Alan also visited many private and public gardens in England and France. These experiences made so strong an impression on him that, while most of his peers were deciding whether to go to Cambridge or Oxford, he was planning to train in horticulture. In 1925, when he was only sixteen, he entered an apprenticeship at the Hughes Glasshouse Nurseries in Dorset, under Emil Hartmann, a skilled market gardener who was then in his midsixties. The Hughes firm specialized in tomatoes, lettuce, and other salad crops, as well as chrysanthemums and carnations of the old, intensely fragrant Malmaison type. Alan concentrated on learning the commercial methods of producing these flowers.

A year later, having heard about the French gardener Louis Lorette, Alan accompanied his parents to Paris and stayed on to study at the Lorette nurseries in St. Cloud. Lorette had developed a complicated but effective technique of summer pruning through which he was able to induce fruit trees to bear abnormally high yields, the fruit being so plentiful as to almost hide the leaves, particularly in pear trees. While in France, Alan also visited the vegetable and fruit gardens at Versailles, a place that represents a high point in the history of intensive production, under the direction of Jean de la Quintinie, gardener to Louis XIV.

By 1927, Alan had returned to the southern coast of England to pursue a second apprenticeship at another Dorset market garden, Haskins Flower Nurseries and Glasshouses. In the 1920s, the characteristic feature of an intensive market garden was its abundance of glass. In order to compete against the produce brought in by rail from more distant, less expensive acreage, intensive gardeners located close to urban centers turned more and more to the use of cold frames and cloches (explained further in chapter 11) to raise the out-of-season specialty crops that fetched higher prices at the market.

Throughout his life, Alan was impetuous, and in the following year his career took a sudden but hardly inappropriate turn. As Alan himself told it, in an interview called "Garden Song"* filmed near the end of his life, he went to

*Available from Bullfrog Films, Oley, PA 19547

see a play one day and was so captivated by the medium that he decided on the spot to become an actor. And he did in fact proceed to train, both for the opera, as a bass baritone at the Carl Rosa Opera Company, and for the theater — he took lessons from one of the leading figures in twentieth-century English drama, Elsie Fogerty.

Miss Fogerty's Central School for Speech Training and Dramatic Art was the embryo of England's National Theatre, as well as the training ground for many great actors, including Olivier, Gielgud, Peggy Ashcroft, and Ann Todd. Students at the Central School during the years that Alan is likely to have attended staged plays by Bernard Shaw and performed as the chorus in T. S. Eliot's *Murder in the Cathedral*, among other productions.

Miss Fogerty was, by all accounts, much like Alan and may well have served as a model for him in many respects. She too was eccentric in manner and dress, passionate in her love of the dramatic moment, and she could be shockingly direct. Above all, she transmitted to her students a deep love of her craft.

Throughout the 1930s, repertory theater was Alan's life. He appeared in contemporary plays like *Rebecca, Petrified Forest,* and *Abraham Lincoln,* often in the lead role, and toured rural Ireland with the Shakespearean Company of one of the last and best known of the great English actor-managers, Anew McMaster.

Shakespeare became a touchstone for Alan for the rest of his life. In his garden talks in Santa Cruz, he often recited soliloquies from the plays. Friar Lawrence's speech in *Romeo and Juliet* — "O, mickle [great] is the powerful grace that lies/In plants, herbs, stones, and their true qualities" — was a favorite, for obvious reasons. Alan was perceived as something of a character at Santa Cruz, and it only added to his reputation when he, a gardener and dirtbuilder, gave Shakespearean readings on the campus and appeared in a play as, no less, a madman.

As World War I had changed Miss Jekyll's life, so World War II disrupted Alan's. At first, because of his pacifist upbringing, he stayed out of military service as a conscientious objector and continued with his theater career. A fellow actor, Richard O'Donoghue, now Registrar at the Royal Academy of Dramatic Art, performed with Alan in the Hull repertory company in 1940, with German bombs falling nightly all around them. According to O'Donoghue, Alan was at that time sensitive and yet full of humor, inclined to such mischief as telling risqué jokes under his breath while on stage, to provoke his younger colleague to laughter in midsentence. Alan kept a dartboard in the dressing room that he and O'Donoghue shared, and the two were used to playing a game during the intermission.

O'Donoghue remembers Alan as a striking figure — tall, with a shock of thick black hair and a piercing gaze. Rustling a billfold full of five-pound notes, obtained from a stockbroker friend, Alan was fond of entertaining Richard and other friends with occasional repasts at a local hotel, a welcome break from the fare provided by their meager actor's pay. After a play, Alan often headed back to the flat that he shared with O'Donoghue and an actress, to pass the night listening to classical music, playing whist, and smoking cigars.

As the war grew worse, Alan's pacifist scruples gave way to his patriotism, and he joined the Royal Navy as a cadet trainee on a minesweeper. He was then just over thirty years old. Posted to India, he was stationed in Bombay and soon worked his way up to the command of a corvette (similar to the U.S. Navy's PT boat). There his legendary temper once got him in trouble. Upset over something, he threw a copy of the *Koran* across the deck, causing his Indian crew, Muslims all, to promptly go on strike. Only a public apology enabled Alan to regain his command.

When the war ended, Alan returned to England and repertory work on the south coast for a couple of years before deciding, in about 1950, to join the National Theater Organization starting up in South Africa. Although he had no use for apartheid and little enthusiasm for constant touring, the open air, dramatic landscape, and rich flora of South Africa appealed to him greatly. As his good friend Freya von Moltke told me, "He disliked so much living in sordid or little hotels on his tours that he often put up a tent somewhere in the open and spent the night there. And the open is just round the corner in all these small towns, where they used to play."

And then along came a chance to garden again. In 1952 or so, he took the job of head gardener at the Admiralty House in Simon's Town, then the residence of Vice Admiral Peveril William-Powlett. In the age of sea power, the Cape peninsula was one of the most important strategic positions in the world, and Simon's Town was the headquarters of the British South Atlantic Command.

The formal gardens at Admiralty House were, when Alan took them over, more than 150 years old. Meticulously kept, they were used for official receptions and entertaining guests of state. Like Golden Gate Park in San Francisco, the land they are built on was originally sand dunes: their very existence is a testament to the skill of the original gardeners. Today, large milkwood trees to the east of the big, white, Dutch-style main house are striking vestiges of the indigenous coastal vegetation. The gardens are a remarkable mixture of native and imported garden plants: *Plumbago auricu-*

lata and bird-of-paradise flowers, endemic to South Africa, flourish alongside hydrangeas, bedding roses, and bougainvillea. (The bird-of-paradise plant, *Strelitzia reginae*, was named in honor of Charlotte of Mecklenburg-Strelitzia, Queen to England's George III when, in 1814, Admiralty House first became the official residence of His Majesty's naval commander-in-chief there.)

In the late 1950s, in anticipation of South African independence, which took place in 1961, England vacated Admiralty House. A British presence was maintained in the area, though, and the Vice Admiral then in charge, Sir Geoffrey Robson, took Alan along with him when he moved to the new official residence, up the coast on Wynberg Hill, in 1957. Here, to the best of my knowledge, is where Alan first created a major garden.

From the house at the crest of Wynberg Hill, the land slopes gently downward to False Bay below. Across the face

Admiralty House gardens

of the hillside Alan dug deep, wide beds, establishing a series of terraces whose effect is both formal and lush. Freya von Moltke visited him there and recalls that "Alan's cottage . . . was perched on a rock about 100 metres above the sea. The shore is mostly flat, white sand and strong waves, but opposite . . . at the other side, east, are big rocky mountains. The sun must rise above them. . . . Alan said that animals visited him in that cottage at night without any timidity. He could have left his windows and doors open at night during the warm season, which is long in South Africa." Alan did have an affinity with wild animals and was good at imitating bird calls — I can remember him quacking just like a duck.

But South Africa couldn't hold him, eventually, and after nearly a decade of acting and gardening there, he left, sailing for the Bahamas in 1959 to work in the gardens of a private estate. From there he was hired to take up a similar position in Long Island, and thus in the early 1960s came to the United States for the first time.

Alan soon found, however, that New York winters were hard on his back, which had been injured twice, once during the war and then again in South Africa, while he was playing a game that is something like our leapfrog. By 1965, he was longing for a change, for a warm place where he could again live close to nature. After getting in touch with his brother Seddon for the first time in many years, Alan decided to try Australia and New Zealand. Seddon was to arrange introductions to friends and relatives there.

Before he left, Alan again contacted Freya, who was then living in Vermont. After warning him that he might not like Australia, she told him she was herself planning to be in California in the fall of 1966. Her friend the philosopher Eugen Rosenstock-Huessy was to be lecturing at a new campus of the University of California, in Santa Cruz. Situated on over 100 acres of former ranchland in the hills overlooking Monterey Bay, the campus, Freya had heard, was an oasis of grassland meadows, wildflowers, and groves of coast redwoods. Tempered by the nearby ocean and low-lying fogs, the climate was mild, Mediterranean. Prophetically, Freya commented that Alan might like working there.

About one year later, in the spring of 1967, Freya was indeed in Santa Cruz, having lunch with philosophy professor Paul Lee. An effort to start a garden on the campus was afoot, one that had attracted many supporters. Students, faculty, and staff alike shared a common appreciation for the superb natural beauty of the site. The first chancellor at Santa Cruz, Dean E. McHenry, a former farm boy from Lompoc, California, had instituted a rule prohibiting any tree larger than ten inches in diameter to be felled without his approval. As a result, roads and footpaths on the campus wind around trees, and the single road leading to and from McHenry Library is only one lane wide.

Another catalyzing force was a talk on the Welsh poet David Jones, given by visiting professor Donald Nichol. Nichol suggested that the campus could give form to its affection for the genius of its place in three ways: a bell within whose sound they would live, a statue, and a garden. All that was needed, mused Professor Lee to Freya, was someone to man the spade.

As it happened, Freya had just received a note from Alan. As she had anticipated, he had not found Australia to his liking, and he was on the move again, heading for San Francisco, where he hoped to visit her. At Lee's comment, she replied, "The new gardener is arriving on the first of March."

And so it was that on the appointed day, Freya met Alan at the Embarcadero in San Francisco and drove him back down the peninsula to Santa Cruz, with his sea chest full of naval uniforms, old boxes of theatrical makeup and memorabilia, and a few of the pieces of Puddleston silver and china that his mother had left to him.

They met Paul Lee on the campus near Cowell Fountain. Alan was a bit formal, hesitant even. As Paul Lee remembers it, though, the big hand that enveloped his reassured him that Alan could do the job. After a walking survey of the campus, Alan announced that he had found the right spot for the garden, on a hillside just above Cowell College.

He undoubtedly had many reasons for choosing this location. His proclivity for hillside gardening is one. Another is that it placed the garden at the entrance to the campus, forming a natural symbolic passage to the world of learning. And most important, the view from that spot out across Monterey Bay is very much like the view eastward from the Admiralty House gardens in South Africa across False Bay. Fundamentally, it is a romantic view, one that unites memory and vision.

The very next day, Alan went into the nearby town of Santa Cruz, bought a spade and a wheelbarrow, and with as much élan as he had used in taking up acting, started to dig. For the next two years, without taking a day off, this fifty-eight-year-old man worked from dawn to dusk every day of the week. Those who were there say he worked more heroically than they had ever seen anyone work before. Students who wandered into the garden often stayed to help, even though they were driven tyrannically; the brilliance and intensity of Alan brought them back day after day.

Freya was one of the reasons Alan worked as hard as he did. Her voice was one of the most respected in his life, and she had charged him, upon his arrival in California, with a mission: he was to help offset the dehumanizing forces of the technological age by sharing his love and knowledge of nature with others. Santa Cruz in the 1960s, a haven of countercultural enthusiasm for the natural and the humanistic, was probably one of the most favorable places in the country to initiate such an undertaking.

By the summer of 1969, two years later, the four acres of garden on that hillside had blossomed into rich fertility. From thin soil and poison oak had sprung an almost magical garden that ranged from hollyhocks and artemisias to exquisite vegetables and nectarines. Old-fashioned roses — the rugosas Agnes and Cornelia, the old cabbage rose la Reine Victoria, Columbia, climbing Will Scarlett, Alchemist, Sombreuil, Shot Silk, Crimson Glory, and Madame Alfred Carrière — twined up the railings of a small chalet there. Every week a special basket of produce and flowers was taken to Chancellor McHenry's house. Flowers festooned the offices of the university staff. A covered garden stand across the road from the garden offered food and flowers free for the taking.

Alan soon had dozens of apprentices. Though he had never taught before, he threw himself into cultivating young minds and their gardening skills. His manner of teaching was the simple, classical one of combining practicality and vision. He would first demonstrate how to do something, and then put the student to work doing the same thing. And like the novice monks at Wilfred's Reichenau, students often found that this way of cultivating the earth led to cultivation of their own perceptions.

As always, Alan was nothing if not mercurial. One of his early apprentices, Michael Zander, remembers planting dahlias with him. After digging an especially large hole, and

Alan Chadwick

layering in leaf mold, bone meal, and aged manure as carefully as if they were making a fine French pastry, they would set and water the plant. But by the next time they planted dahlias, the recipe would have changed.

As well as demonstrating garden practice, Alan sought to

communicate vision. Michael and another early student of Alan's, Steve Kaffka, often visited Alan's apartment on Sunday mornings. There they would listen to opera, drink freshly ground coffee (sweetened with Eagle condensed milk), and munch on Alan's blackberry tarts. Alan would talk about gardening and perhaps enact something like the turning of the seasons, beginning with winter.

Hunched over, cupping his hands about his face, he would exhale a long, rasping, shallow breath, instantly creating a vivid image of contraction, sleep, dormant potential. Then, opening his arms into spring, his back would straighten up, his voice begin to sing, a smile play across his face. As he reached summer, his voice would become full, expansive, resonant. His outstretched arms evoked the open sky, his eyes seemed to reflect the full sun. Then, at the word *fall*, his back would bow again, his shoulders bending inward. His eyes would cloud over, his hands and arms curl in across his chest. Drawing in his breath, he would turn his face down and away, as if to shield it from the approaching chill.

Even in play, Alan exhibited the same forceful passion he brought to his garden labors. One of his recreations as a young man had been boxing, and in his cruise chest were a couple of pairs of old trunks. One day he and Professor Lee, a big man, easily outweighing Alan, squared off in a friendly match. Rather than adopting a predictable defensive strategy, avoiding Lee's advantage and hoping to tire him out, Alan's approach was to overwhelm his larger opponent in a matter of seconds with a wild, windmilling, all-out style of attack.

Page Smith, another key supporter of the Santa Cruz garden and at that time Provost of Cowell College, was similarly surprised in a tennis match with Alan. Somewhat taken aback by Alan's unorthodox but highly effective style of play, Smith took his time picking up the balls, which provoked a caustic shout from his partner: "Did you come here to play tennis or what?" Smith stepped up the pace a bit, but it wasn't enough for his passionately competitive opponent. After the next point, Alan jumped over the net and ran around on Smith's side of the court, retrieving the balls himself in a quirky display of one-upmanship.

At the age of sixty, Alan was in exuberant good health. He continued to ride a bicycle, for the sheer joy of it, and generally avoided using automobiles, considering them a threat to humanity. He did, however, own a car, an old blue-gray Rambler that a student had given him. It had the words *This too could be yours* painted on one side.

One day Alan needed to take the car into town. Driving away from the campus, on a downhill road, he evidently picked up too much speed and was pulled over to the side by a policeman. Alan got out, nodded at the legend on the side of his car, and tossed the keys into the startled officer's hand. Nonplussed by this casual approach, the man over-reacted and made the mistake of drawing his revolver. Alan reacted instinctively: a left jab, a quick move, and the gun was first in Alan's hands and then in the weeds by the side of the road.

The matter came to court, of course. Alan made his appearance in a bright blue, double-breasted gabardine suit left over from his theater days. He looked like someone from another century. The judge listened carefully to Alan's story, then turned to the policeman. "Did you pull your gun on this gentleman?" "Yes." "Did he hit you and take it away?" "Yes." "Case dismissed."

In the six years that Alan worked at Santa Cruz, however,

what drew the most attention to him was the garden, in which so much grew with such abundance, and without the use of artificial fertilizers or pesticides. In that period of time, Alan introduced three basic techniques that have since had a strong influence on gardening throughout the United States. The first is the raised bed. A traditional approach, the raised bed (described in detail in chapter 10) is ideal for small-scale intensive gardening, especially using hand tools. Although it was practiced in some biodynamic circles and by Peter Chan (author of *Intensive Gardening the Chinese Way*) at the time, the raised bed was virtually unheard of before 1970 in this country.

Since its inception at Santa Cruz, detailed documentation of the increased productivity and decreased water and fertilizer requirements of raised beds, along with clear instructions on how to establish and maintain them, have been published by another early acquaintance of Chadwick's, John Jeavons, in his book *How to Grow More Vegetables*. The raised-bed technique is now widely promoted in publications ranging from the Troy-Bilt Rototiller catalogue to the Peace Corps' self-sufficient farming manual.

In my view, Alan's second major contribution was his

emphasis on the value of gardening with hand labor and hand tools. By treating gardening as an artistic physical discipline, he rekindled a sense of the joy and dignity of working outdoors. (He also, in part, inspired the founding of Smith & Hawken, now a leading supplier of fine hand tools for the garden.)

Alan's third contribution was his emphasis on the mixed garden. In this he is not unique: backyard gardeners have always liked to grow a mixture of vegetables, herbs, flowers, and fruit. But Alan did it in a special way, one that mixed style and substance.

By 1972, Alan was again ready for something new. In that winter and the following spring, he helped establish two community gardens in California, in Saratoga and in Green Gulch, a Zen Buddhist retreat north of San Francisco. Then he went north, invited by Richard Wilson, a rancher in Mendocino County, to start a garden school in the remote California town of Covelo.

A few apprentices followed Alan to Covelo, bringing with them that same old Rambler, a horsehair mattress Paul Lee had given him, and little else. From what was there in the local leaf mold, barnyard manure, and soil, and from a few seed and plant orders, the project quickly took shape. Soon eight acres were under cultivation, and a growing number of apprentices, reaching forty or more at times, came to study and garden. The same techniques initiated at Santa Cruz — double-digging, hand watering, companion planting, and the emphasis on compost, herbs, and the old-fashioned standard seed varieties — were continued at Covelo. (Double-digging is described on pages 156–157, companion planting on pages 193–194 and 231.) Lorette pruning was introduced as well, and a large, circular herb garden with stone paths was built. An entry from the Covelo log

Planting of Royal Sovereign strawberries in the east garden.

Procedure
1) Remove soil from hole
2) Mix ½ trowel bone meal into the soil at the bottom of the hole
3) Remove 3 trowels of soil. Reserve
4) Place ½ spade of short manure (stockpiled) in hole. Mix well.
5) Replace the soil (from step 1) into the hole. Mix. MAKE a mound.
6) Spread roots –
   Crown should be at ground level but allow for settling.
7) Sift over roots – bone meal and soil mix (from step 3)
8) Sift over this – ⅓ spade of manure
9) Lightly cover the manure with soil.
10) "Bang" them home –– using pressure from foot.
11) Marry edges – lightly – careful of roots

soil
manure
bone meal
+ soil

manure, bone meal, soil

Samedi 17 avril
High clouds ~ overcast all day ~ soft rain at mid day.
· Prepared brassica beds   · Cultivation of lettuce beds
   Light manure – spit turned
· Glass house
   pricked out nicotiana (old tomato flat soil + compost + ⅓ mixture)
· Market → Sold all radishes and beets.
                        (8 bunches)   (6 bunches)
        Sold 6 bunches leeks and 8 bunches of chard.

Covelo logbook entry

book, reproduced here, shows how they planted Royal Sovereign strawberries.

From Covelo it is a two-hour drive to the highway and the next gas station. Movie theaters and other forms of entertainment are equally distant. What made new apprentices find their way to such a remote place and then put up with the rigors of hand cultivation once there? Growing awareness of the crisis in technological agriculture, and a concern for world hunger and for building a sustainable way to produce food were powerful motives. Equally, Alan's charismatic reputation attracted many.

One of them, Fred Marshall, lived in Alan's house for five years at Covelo and served as one of his two aides-de-camp. The day began at 3:30 A.M., when Alan arose to prepare for his morning lecture. Not infrequently, he awoke discouraged by the magnitude of the task before him, the challenge of rebuilding a link between man and nature that he felt had been lost.

Fred would typically begin with the morning ritual of grinding coffee beans. As he did, he would ask questions and report on farm activities, engaging Alan intuitively, discursively. One thing would lead to another, the birds would begin their predawn songs, and Alan's spirits would begin to lift. Soon he would be busily looking up names in reference books, making a few notes, thinking out loud. By the time of his lecture, he would have once again transformed himself into a powerfully persuasive speaker, ready with his lines and his feelings.

The lecture might, for example, be about legumes. These plants are important because they build soil and the bacteria on their roots help "fix" nitrogen, making it available for plants. Alan maintained that these bacteria and the other biological life associated with legumes helped prevent fungus problems in the garden, and he liked to grow a variety of legumes and turn them under, into the beds, a process called "green manuring." By recounting the appearance of a plant and its use in ancient Greece and Rome, as well as its traditional place on English farms and gardens, he was able to communicate a practical, complete picture of its role for his students.

Fava beans (*Vicia fava*) were one of his favorite green manures. This bean has been grown since prehistoric times, as we know from finding evidence of it in the archeological sites of the lake dwellers in Switzerland and at Glastonbury, in England, and was mentioned by Virgil. In ancient cultures, its scent was thought to cause mental disorders, and the white flowers, with their dark purple blotches, were symbolic of funerals. The fragrance is also reputed to be an aphrodisiac, and Alan enjoyed reporting that it was for this reason that friends he had known in Lincolnshire had kept their female servants on the premises when the fields of fava bean were in flower.

In the genus *Vicia* — the vetches — there are about 150 species. *Vicia cracca*, the tufted vetch, is a perennial with bright blue flowers that was traditionally grown in hedgerows. A closely related legume, *Onobrychis viciaefolia*, is, like the vetches, a member of the subfamily *Faboideae*. The Greek word *onos* means "ass," and *brycho* means "to consume greedily" — this plant is not only a soilbuilder but is also obviously excellent fodder. The French peasants who grew it extensively certainly were aware of this: their name for it, *sainfoin*, means "holy hay."

If Covelo represents the zenith of Alan's arc across the 1970s, it also marks the beginning of his decline — here his health began to fail him. The cold winters aggravated his old back problems, making him irritable and harder to work with. New apprentices, who did not know him well, were less tolerant of his eruptions. More ominously, it was learned that he had prostate cancer.

It was clear he needed better weather and a different situation. Feeling a mixture of hope and dejection, almost as though exiled, Alan traveled south, settling for a short time in Sonoma, California, still looking for a place to build another garden and school. In a letter written February 1, 1978, to his friend Father Michael Culligan, he describes one brief prospect:

> The dream: known as the spa of 1850, the Soda Springs. A superb facade of mountains, perfect soils, escalations. A veritable Cote d'Azur setting. Stream and waterfall, *and* all the buildings solid stone. The entire project in skeleton. Burned out in 1925, the timber all gone, stone almost all in perfect

condition, sitting, waiting, for . . . What a prayer answered! Housing for all, hostel, clinique. And beyond all dreams, a colossal rotunda, used as a ballroom.

Also a large wooden house, unburdened, for immediate use. And the bubbling spa waters, like to Vichy. This is all beyond belief. Richard [Wilson] flew down and saw it. I feel he thinks it vastly too, too much.

We do not so regard it, and the Sonoma persons are vastly excited also. It is really all-the-year-round growing. What more perfect for the staff and students?

One building lends itself vitally to a chapel. We're pursuing all out and to have a meeting with the new owner. Any terms are obvious to agree to. It must come off! . . .

Our warmest greetings to you,
Chadwick.

The project did not come off. The property was not, in fact, for sale. Alan's health and hopes worsened daily.

There was to be one more chimera. Hearing about a religious community in New Market, Virginia, that had just purchased 1,300 acres of land with the intention of making a garden on it, Alan wrote to them. Upon receiving an encouraging reply, he embarked on a last, desperate venture.

His friends at Covelo were more than helpful. They loaded a semi truck so full of plants and greenhouse glass the driver almost refused to take it. But the three-year-old black currants, the eighteen-inch-wide asparagus roots, and the four-year-old perennial flowers all made it from one coast to the other, and in the winter of 1978–79 in the mild climate of the upper South, Alan planted what amounted to a ready-made garden. But the overnight magic was short-lived.

The following fall the New Market group fell delinquent

in its payments on the land, and the project came to an abrupt halt. Alan's cancer had by then become "impossibly painful," as he wrote to a friend, and he needed a nurse. Death was approaching, and it looked as though he had no place to go.

A young woman at the New Market garden, Acacia Downs, then took on the job of caring for Alan. For a short time they lived in a house in Virginia, out of sight of the fields where the garden had been and where cattle now grazed. Freya visited, as did Richard Wilson. Quickly, places were located where Alan might pass his final hours, including the Findhorn Institute in Scotland and a monastery in the mountains near the Mojave Desert in California. But Alan chose, at the invitation of abbot Richard Baker, to return to Green Gulch.

From November 1979 until the middle of the following year, Alan and Acacia lived at the Wainwright Center at Green Gulch, in a cottage set in a grove of redwood and Monterey pine. Alan ate little and seldom went outside. Every day, flowers from the garden he had inspired were brought to his room. He and Acacia looked over his favorite art books. To feel that he was a part of the Green Gulch community, he gave lectures three or four times a week on various topics such as roses, garden technique, and his spiritual views.

Before he left Virginia, Alan had asked Acacia to give away or otherwise dispose of many of his things, including paintings, letters, clothes, etc., because he didn't want people "chasing the name of Alan Chadwick." In his last months, his underlying tenderness came to the fore. Not that his temper completely disappeared, however. One day, while reading to him, Acacia picked up a pear she had

View from Alan's rock

brought with her and casually took a bite out of it. Alan instantly rose up in his bed, raging at her. "You beast!" he shouted. "How can you insult the gift of food so?" And then in explanation, "A pear such as that should be held before your eyes. Its fragrance should be savored and its form admired before you bite into it, my dear. Don't you know this pear is the culmination of centuries of man and nature cultivating each other? It is a gift and a precious delight. Do not spoil it with carelessness."

Alan died on May 25, 1980. His funeral was as extraordinary as his life. Hundreds of people gathered at Green Gulch for it. Father Culligan wore his ceremonial robes, burned incense, and chanted the ritualistic Latin that Alan adored. Richard Baker conducted a Buddhist ceremony and erected a stone to commemorate Alan that looks out over the Pacific.

Father Culligan, who knew Alan's old world of cathedral, hedgerow, and plays in small towns in rural Ireland, and who often walked along northern California beaches with him, remembers Alan this way:

That was the place to meet Alan Chadwick. Not in a room, but [with] the little birds running along the strand, the foam, the fog, the mist, and the Burberries up around our ears, there he'd talk about modern man.

Then he'd stop and gaze out, with that gaze he had. He'd look out with that craggy, rocky countenance, and gaze into the horizon with the seagulls squawking around us and the smell of the seaweed, into the timelessness of the sea.

Alan's legacy, especially the use of raised beds and French intensive planting, has become so popular as to be almost routine today. The garden he started at Santa Cruz is still going strong; it now serves as the nucleus for an accredited Agroecology program (see the listing in appendix A), where research into allelopathy, or companion planting, is being carried out.

PART THREE

The Practice of Gardening

Thinking Like a Seed

The first step in starting a garden, as you might guess, is understanding and appreciating what's already there. Like every good gardener, you first observe the genius of the place — its light, air, earth, and water. And you do this from the point of view of the seed that you intend to germinate and the plant you want to grow in those conditions. Plants are individuals, and you must take their proclivities into account when you begin a garden.

Go outside and walk around in your garden site. Or better yet, put a chair out there and sit for a while, when the weather's fine, taking it in. Any garden must, to be successful, build on the natural circumstances of its location. And there is always a bit of a tradeoff involved: a site that gets lots of sun may be a little too dry; one with good soil and plenty of water may lie at the bottom of a hill, where cold air collects. But don't let these problems deter you — you'll never find the ideal place.

Remember in thinking like a seed to take the point of view of an embryonic plant about to spring into life. What you want to know, from this perspective, are things like: Is this soil warm enough for me? Will I get enough air, sunlight, water, and nutrients? Or will I get cold earth, soggy feet, too much shade or too much sun, and an inadequate larder? Will it be windy or calm out there? Will the air be pure and fresh, or full of dust and pollutants?

Light

Think first about the sun. Your garden should be situated where it will get six to eight hours of full sunlight a day, particularly if you're going to be growing vegetables. (Remember that in spring and fall, trees and buildings cast longer shadows than in summer.) In some parts of the country this will be an easy condition to satisfy; in others, it won't. In Colorado, I get bright sun most of the year, with thin mountain air and few clouds. This makes it easy to find places that get enough sun for a garden, but, as always, there's a price to pay: it's harder to find places to grow those plants that prefer shade and moisture. As you can imagine, in the forests of the Northeast and the Northwest much the opposite conditions prevail: there shade and moisture abound, but open, sunny garden spots are at a premium.

Air

The second thing to consider is the air and the climate, particularly those times of the year when the temperature drops below freezing. The low point of the year is the winter solstice, which falls on or about the twenty-first of December. This is the shortest day of the year. The earth is still, dormant, slumbering. After that, the daylengths slowly increase. On about March 21, the first day of spring, the vernal equinox occurs, one of the two times each year when the lengths of day and night are equal. Sensing the growing tides of light and warmth, seeds germinate now. In the next few months, the earth bursts into bloom. Life courses into every vein, root, and leaf. A crescendo is reached at the summer solstice, the longest day of the year, June 21. Then, inexorably, the tide turns once more and life begins to ebb. By the autumnal equinox, in September, the harvest is mostly behind us, and the Northern Hemisphere is slowly settling down for another winter's sleep.

Plants vary in their "hardiness," that is, their ability to withstand cold temperatures. When the temperature of the air — and thus the ground — drops in the fall, most plants die back or go dormant. By the same token, if seeds are put in the ground too early in the spring, they won't germinate. The roots of young plants will have difficulty drawing water and nutrients out of the chilly earth. Even if they do get started, an unseasonably late frost can crumple and blacken their tender leaves, giving you a replanting job.

On the other hand, some plants not only can stand the cold, they actually prefer or even insist on it, and won't do well at all if you wait too long to get their seed (or transplants, which are discussed in chapter 11) into the soil.

As your gardening experience grows, you'll soon come to know which plants thrive in the cold and which insist on warmth. Most leafy, salad vegetables, such as lettuce, spinach, swiss chard, and the cabbage tribe, like cool weather and can stand some frost. Roots and onion-family plants fall into this category too. Many woody-stemmed garden plants, such as raspberries and apples, also want to have a cold period. As a general rule, however, plants with soft stems that we harvest for their fruit, the "tender" summer crops, such as melons, squash, and tomatoes, like warm weather and die when it freezes.

The best growing season is broadly defined by the length of time between the last frost in spring and the first frost in the fall. Your local county extension agent or garden store can usually give you the dates of the first and last frosts, as well as information on the relative hardiness or tenderness of many plants commonly grown in your area. Tender plants like tomatoes, beans, zinnias, and many other annuals can only be put in the ground when all danger of frost is safely past. (Annuals are plants with a one-year life cycle.) Hardier plants — lettuce is a good example — can be

planted earlier, because a little chilling not only doesn't hurt them, but may actually help them grow stronger and tastier. Melons, on the other hand, need a long, hot summer and are not something you would want to attempt to raise in, say, a mountain climate with a short growing season of only ninety days or fewer.

Think also about moving air, the wind. Strong winds are one of the most severe challenges a plant can face. They not only dry out the leaves and the soil, but also break branches, blow down fruit, and carry sprinkler water miles in the wrong direction. If your site is exposed to such winds, you will need to protect it with a sturdy fence or hedge.

If you plan to garden in a hilly area, remember that cold air, like water, tends to flow downhill and collect in low-lying hollows and valleys, as well as behind obstacles like walls and fences. This is why gardens in low spots have more problems with late frosts than others in the same vicinity.

Unfortunately, you will also have to think about air pollution, especially in metropolitan areas. Near heavily traveled roads, you will need to consider the possibility of contamination by airborne particulates of lead, which can accumulate in soil, leaves, and human beings to toxic levels. (Lead also gets into the soil around older buildings that were painted with lead-based paints.) Local public health departments and extension agents can usually help you determine whether your garden site should be sampled for lead pollution. Air pollutants limit the varieties of trees and shrubs that grow well in cities, and now acid rain also kills some plants. On the positive side, the warmer wind-protected microclimate of cities will support plants that normally are not hardy in your area.

Earth

Third, consider the earth itself, specifically the soil at your site. If it is already growing something, even if it's just grass or weeds, then it will also grow a garden. But if the only thing you've ever seen there is bare ground, then something may be wrong, something that should be corrected before the first seed or plant goes in. It may be a lack of nutrients or water, or it may be something else — a lingering herbicide may have been applied there, old crankcase oil may have been dumped there, something may have been mixed with the soil that will prevent anything from growing there. Or the soil may simply be so compacted that roots won't survive, in which case organic matter mixed in will take care of the problem. (See chapter 10.)

If you want to learn more about your soil, a good step to take is to have a soil test done. This is a simple process that is performed routinely and inexpensively all across the country, usually under the auspices of agricultural extension agencies.

The two major things you will learn from a soil test are whether your site is deficient in any of the three main plant nutrients — N (nitrogen), P (phosphorus), or K (potassium) — and whether your soil is "sweet" (alkaline) or "sour" (acid). If your soil is deficient in N, P, or K, you can add the missing ingredient(s) in either artificial or — and this is my choice — organic form. Artificial fertilizers are widely sold in garden stores, hardware stores, and supermarkets. Most contain all three basic ingredients, in relative proportions indicated by a set of numerals on the container, such as 5-10-5. (The first number gives the percentage of nitrogen in the mixture, the second the amount of phosphorus, and the third the level of potassium.)

132

In very general terms, nitrogen is needed for the growth of strong, healthy leaves, phosphorus helps fruits and flowers develop properly, and potassium promotes sturdy root growth. If you use artificial fertilizers, choose either an evenly balanced mixture of all three, or one containing a larger amount of the particular substance needed by your soil. The soil test will also tell the recommended amount.

I hasten to add, however, that a good compost will do the same job of supplying nutrients, and with much more sensitivity to the needs of soil and crop life than you can ever determine consciously. The criticism is sometimes made of compost that it doesn't contain enough plant nutrients to be effective. My feeling is just the opposite: chemicals tend to give too much of a narrow selection of nutrients to plants. Too much nitrogen, for instance, can actually be detrimental to plants because it encourages fast but tender, weak growth that is more susceptible to frost damage, insects, and disease, as well as producing plants that are watery and less flavorful.

Adding compost or manure to your soil also adds texture in the form of organic matter. Organic matter and its nutrients are worked and consumed by soil organisms and replenished by their own wastes and bodies when they die. A good soil texture creates a beneficial environment for soil organisms, and that's where the best nutrition of all comes from — the cycle of life and death of both the visible and the invisible organisms present in a healthy soil community. "Two-thirds of the question of fertility," Alan liked to say, "is soil texture."

Also, when a well-composted soil is watered, nutrients are neither leached straight down nor kept locked into its particles, as tends to happen with sandy or clayey soils. Even from the viewpoint of simple efficiency, it's much easier to add compost, get the soil texture right, then let the nutrients follow.

In sum, the overall effect of compost is to create a soil that behaves like a sponge, holding nutrients in a gentle suspension until they are needed. The result is a true soil culture, one that neither over- nor understimulates plants. (There are places in the United States that will specifically test your soil for its organic content. The address of one, Wood's End Laboratory, is given in appendix B.)

The second thing you'll learn from a soil test is whether your soil is too acid or too alkaline, and this will be indicated in terms of its pH. The symbol *pH* stands for *p*otential *H*ydrogen. A pH of 7 is neutral; higher numbers indicate increasing alkalinity, lower number increasing acidity. The pH of soil is significant because it is associated with the ability of soil particles to hold and release nutrients. In nature, pH values vary widely and plants become adapted to extremes. Ferns, as a rule, like very acid soils; cacti prefer them quite alkaline. Most garden plants, however, have been developed in managed environments that tend to have a slightly acid pH of 6 to 7. Soils that are more acid, as those in the eastern United States tend to be, or those that are alkaline, as those in the West tend to be, need some amendment to make them suitable for garden culture.

The direct method of adjusting soil pH is to add lime to acid places and sulfur to those that are too alkaline. My approach to these conditions is to combine compost with lime in the former, and to use compost by itself in the latter. Here another one of compost's virtues — its ability to neutralize pH — becomes evident. Composting, in short, is the all-around elegant alternative. Exactly how it works to adjust pH is something of a mystery, but we know that it has much to do with the presence of life in the soil. Earthworms, for example, help make an acid soil more alkaline just through their normal processes of ingestion and excretion.

You can get a good feel for the kind of soil you have at your site just by picking up a handful of it and gently squeezing it, as I did on the Adirondacks walk in chapter 2. If it keeps its shape when you squeeze it and let go, then you know it's not too sandy. If it crumbles when you next stroke it with your thumb, you also know it's not too clayey.

The main way in which the three basic soil types — sandy, clayey, and silt — are differentiated by soil scientists is by the average size of their particles. Clay soils are composed of the smallest particles, some 1/1200 of an inch in diameter or less. Sandy soils, at the other end of the spectrum, have particles running a thousand times or so as large, about 1/12 of an inch. In between is silt. Loam, a general name for the ideal garden soil, is made up of about equal parts of all three soil types, plus organic matter. A loamy soil is the best place for a seed to germinate and a plant to grow. It has an available store of nutrients and a loose texture through which the warm, moist gases of oxidation and decomposition can circulate. Roots can penetrate down into the soil depths, which are relatively free from fluctuations of hot and cold, moist and dry, found nearer the surface.

Water

Last but hardly least, give some thought to water. Find out how much precipitation falls in your location annually, and when. My Colorado garden gets relatively little precipitation, perhaps ten to fourteen inches a year. (Twice that is usually considered the ideal amount.) What's more, it mainly falls in the late winter and early spring, and in the form of snow, rather than being evenly distributed throughout the year. True, this does provide me with a spring reservoir, a moisture bank of sorts in the soil that is slowly withdrawn by capillary action as the ground warms and dries. But we also have a long, hot, dry summer where I live, and those reserves are soon depleted, long before the growing season is over. So, out comes the sprinkler for daily use until I put the beds to rest again in the fall. The spongy effect of compost is a great help in circumstances like mine, since it is a way of helping even out the swings between a wet snowmelt and bone-dry ground.

It is also a good idea to begin keeping a garden notebook at this stage. This need be nothing more than a manila folder in which you file useful tidbits such as fact sheets from the county extension agent, notes on frost dates and precipitation rates, addresses, catalogues, and so on. As your garden experience grows, this notebook will become a journal and a log, in which you begin recording planting dates, notes on the weather, the names of plants you may want to grow again next year, and so forth. These comments come in handy later, as time goes by and memory fades.

Finally, as you contemplate getting started, don't forget that your city, town, or neighborhood has its own Chadwicks, Jekylls, Wilfreds, and Olmsteds, its own local gardening maestros, who already understand the special needs of the seeds and the plants where you live. Many of the questions you will ask about your garden have been asked and answered (in a variety of ways) many times before. When you take a turn around the block, keep an eye out for signs of experienced gardeners. And when you find them, don't hesitate to make their acquaintance. About the only thing gardeners like better than coaxing something out of the ground is a chance to share their triumphs and failures with a fellow cultivator.

Here is an exercise that will give you a hands-on feeling for sun, air, earth, and moisture, and their importance to the seed. Whether you decide to make a garden or not, this exercise will let you start a seed, put the plant in the ground, and from then on admire gardens as an insider.

Choose a native wildflower or common vegetable, something that is not too difficult to germinate. Any annual cut flower or table vegetable common in your area will be easy to germinate. But it will be more interesting in the long run if you can germinate a perennial plant, simply because it will return year after year. Your state flower, even certain flowering trees or shrubs, may be good candidates. Garden stores often carry packets of native wildflowers that sprout readily. Ask someone in the store or a local gardener to recommend an indigenous plant that germinates readily.

My state flower, the columbine, is not difficult to start and makes as lovely a plant in the garden as in the mountains, its native habitat. A neighboring state, Kansas, honors the sunflower, an annual which is even easier to get started. If you live in Virginia, however, where the lady slipper is the state flower, you would be well advised to buy one that is already started, or try something else. Plants vary in their willingness to face the world.

To learn something about the sun, air, earth, and water requirements of the plant you've chosen, look up its native home in a garden encyclopedia. The sunflower, for example, stands out in the full midwestern sun on a thick stalk that bears up to the open prairie wind. My mountain columbines like the half-day shade of a rocky outcropping, plus mountain grit, a humusy mulch, and fresh-flowing snowmelt.

Next you'll need a container and some soil mix, a place with adequate light (a south-facing window in the winter), and a watering can to apply tepid water gently. As a planting mix, most plants will be happy with the basic triumvirate of leafy compost, loamy soil, and sand. Sunflowers, for example, often pop up along roadside ditches where grasses, weeds, and leaves fall and decay to make a rough compost. To gather some of this material, walk into an undisturbed, shady place where there are lots of deciduous trees, brush away the whole leaves on the surface of the ground, and just gather up a few handfuls of the sweet-smelling, mostly decayed leaf underneath that looks almost like soil.

Beneath that, dig up a spadeful of real dirt. It should be stickier, harder to dig, more packed together. The third ingredient, sand, can often be found nearby as well, where a stream or river makes a bend, or from a local playground. Make sure it's dry.

Now sift the three soil components separately through a coarse flour sifter or other ¼-inch screen. Then mix equal portions of each together. You can also buy a comparable mix at a nursery or garden store, but it will be made of ingredients like peat moss and vermiculite rather than leaf, soil, and sand.

Fill a 4-inch clay flower pot with your soil mix. Brush off excess soil until the mix is just level with the top of the pot. Now press the soil down ½ inch with the bottom of a water glass to compress it. This aids the capillary action that helps draw moisture and nutrients up from the lower soil levels to the top, where the seed lies.

Sow five or six seeds into the pressed soil. Don't expect all of them to germinate. Resift some of the leftover mix so that it becomes very fine and free of lumps. With this soil,

Seed-planting exercise

cover the seed to a depth that is twice its diameter, and very lightly press this soil down as well.

Water with room-temperature water. Use a watering can that makes a fine shower of small drops. *Do not* wash away the soil covering the seed. As an alternative, you can also water from the bottom of the pot by setting it in a basin of room-temperature water, allowing the water to move up through the soil by capillarity. At the first sign of dampness at the top of the pot, remove it from the basin — again, be careful not to wash or float the top covering away.

Keep the seeds moist until they germinate by watering occasionally. You can water less often if you cover the pot with plastic wrap or a piece of glass to reduce transpiration. I prefer, however, more frequent watering because the covering technique cuts off air and thus increases the chance of fungus disease. Until the seeds germinate, keep the pot in a shady place to cut down on water loss.

The seeds now have earth, water, and air circulation. Another consideration pertaining to air is the temperature in the soil. As a general rule, 60 to 70 degrees is a good germinating temperature; a warm room in your home will usually do just fine.

As soon as the shoots peek out from the soil, move the pot to a sunny windowsill. Now light becomes extremely important, for it is only in the presence of light that a plant has the capacity to convert soil, water, and air into food through the process of photosynthesis. If several seeds germinate, transplant the seedlings to individual pots as they become crowded. Or ruthlessly remove all but the two healthiest ones.

A few weeks (or months) later, when your seedlings are strong and the weather is warm enough, take your flower pot outside to a place where the plants can flourish, a spot like one they would do well in, in the wild. Dig a hole somewhat larger than the flower pot and turn the plant out, soil and all, into your hand, being careful to rest the stem between your index and middle fingers. Set the roots into the hole and fill it with the soil that you removed. Bring water, and soak in well.

If the spot is in full sun or the weather is dry, come by every day with water until the plant is no longer wilting when you arrive. Cut your visits to every other day, then weekly. Finally, let it go. If you chose an annual, you'll know you picked the right combination of conditions for that plant when you check back later in the year and find it blooming and healthy. If you chose a perennial, you can come back in a year, a decade, or more to see its progress.

The Basic Cycle: Year 1

Starting a garden can seem like an overwhelming project. There are so many things to think of, so many things to take care of, and imagination grows faster than a weed. The first thing to do is take your time. Step back from the excitement of planning and getting ready. Don't try to figure it all out at once. Remember, the earth is already a garden. It already works. All you have to do is *cultivate* that basic fact.

Remember too that human beings have been gardening for thousands of years. We have a basic feel for the earth. You can also draw on the traditions of the great garden masters to learn successful garden practices.

In this chapter I describe the basic cycle of making a garden. It consists of ten basic steps that follow one after another as regularly and naturally as the seasons. Each step is described in some detail. If you're new to gardening, you should probably follow each step closely at first. As time passes, however, you'll want to play your own variations on this basic rhythm. The ten steps are:

1. Buy good tools and materials.
2. Prepare the ground.

3. Make fall compost.
4. Plan the garden.
5. Plant the garden.
6. Make spring compost.
7. Cultivate the garden.
8. Observe the garden.
9. Control pests.
10. Harvest.

1. Buy good tools and materials.

I recommend getting a garden fork, a spade, a hoe, a trowel, a hose with sprinkler attachments, a rake, a pair of hand pruners (secateurs), a pruning saw, and a sturdy, heavy-duty wheelbarrow. That will do, to start with. Also, buy or gather some aged manure, bone meal, leaf mold, and wood ash.

Tools that are admirable in and of themselves will set the right tone of craftsmanship in your digging, pruning, and watering. When you step on the heel of a good spade, it slips into the soil cleanly. Sharp pruners make a cut that is healthy and heals rapidly, deterring pests, disease, and impaired plant function. A dull blade just tears and saws at the unhappy limb, inviting pests, disease, etc.

I buy most of my tools from Smith & Hawken, a firm that carries the time-honored English Bulldog brand. The initial outlay for fine tools will be a bit higher than for other brands, but they are well worth it.

It's also possible, of course, to find good Yankee tools, especially if you haunt farm and yard sales. I have an old spade that I bought for $2.00 many years ago in Arkansas. The handle is sturdy post oak and a steel reinforcing strap rises halfway up the shaft. It was built to last, and it has.

Once you have good tools, you'll want to care for them.

In Alan's garden, we cleaned them after every chore: a quick scrape with the "wood man," a piece of beveled-edge wood with a handle, to remove encrusted soil from spade or fork, then a light pass with a wire brush dipped in water, a no. 9 hand file to keep a straight, sharp edge, and finally a quick thrust or two into a box of sand mixed with old crankcase oil to prevent rusting. The next time we wanted to take it out into the garden, the tool was there, clean, sharp, ready for use.

The first year you'll also need to buy some aged manure. (By the second year, you'll be relying on your own compost instead.) You may hear that good manure can't be found in the city, and it is true that there aren't many cows in downtown Manhattan, or horses. But in the suburbs and smaller towns, wherever there are yards big enough for a vegetable patch, barnyard manure is usually not far away. Where I live, a very cosmopolitan community of 85,000 residents, it's easy to buy manure. Dairies and stables will often deliver as well, if you're ordering more than a small amount. Be sure to get aged manure, which is at least six months old.

In the past, gardeners preferred to use ground bone meal, straight from the slaughter house. Nowadays, steamed must do.

Leaf mold, which is nothing more than decayed leaves, can usually be had free for the asking and gathering. Use deciduous leaves only, not evergreen needles, which are too acid. Oak is the caviar of leaf mold, beech the next most desirable.

If you have nothing else, no compost, no manure, no leaf mold, you can use peat moss. Peat moss will help improve the texture of your soil, opening it up so that air, water, nutrients, and roots can move through it freely. But that's about all it will do. Peat moss will not add nutrients or beneficial microorganisms to the soil, as all these other supplements will. If you have to use peat moss, make sure it's springy (hold some in your hand and squeeze it) and has good fiber content. Some commercial peat moss is so fine and powdery it's not worth buying and turning into the ground.

A rich source of potassium, wood ash can be obtained from your own or a neighbor's fireplace and mixed sparingly into your beds or compost piles. Avoid the ash of plastics or the color pages in magazines and Sunday papers.

Should you use artificial fertilizers? Over the long run, as your soil develops into a fine, humusy loam, with plenty of organic matter and lots of life in it, you won't need them at all. If you're careful about rotating your crops so that you don't one-sidedly deplete nutrients, and you return a wide range of elements back to the soil through composting, growing legumes, or adding manure, artificial fertilizers are extraneous.

I don't use artificials in my own garden, and I don't recommend them. Even used sparingly they can have subtly deleterious effects on your plants. By kicking up growth, the nitrogen they add can produce a crop that looks big, green, and succulent, but which is in fact soft and watery and not as healthy as one allowed to grow at a slower, but more natural pace. And unfortunately, those soft, watery leaves are the kind of food that insects adore. By introducing artificial fertilizers into your garden, you may find that you have inadvertently set off down the wrong kind of garden path, one that leads to ever-increasing amounts of pesticides and similar, avoidable chemical exigencies. Also, by feeding your plants a diet of artificial fertilizers, you shortcut the microbial processes that make nutrients available to plants in nature. If those microbes don't get the organic wastes they feed on, they die, and this is the opposite of what you want to have happening in your garden soil. By using organic supplements instead of artificial fertilizers, you're much more likely to create a thriving subterranean community of soil organisms.

And finally, artificials are made from petrochemicals. They will not always be so cheap — they're already a cost problem for farmers. Learning to recycle organic wastes for fertility is a more sustainable way to garden in the long run.

However, in the short run, using a balanced, complete artificial fertilizer can be helpful. Artificials will almost certainly increase your vegetable production in the first few years. Many gardeners, and better gardeners than I am, use artificials. They are labor-saving and readily available. If you do use them, add organic matter at the same time, though, since even artificial fertilizers will quickly leach out of the soil unless they have a humusy sponge to cling to.

Also make sure, if you do use an artificial fertilizer, to pick one that provides a balanced foundation of nitrogen, phosphorus, and potassium for your crops and soil conditions. (The label on the container must indicate these percentages. A soil test will quickly inform you of any nutrient deficits in your soil.)

Organic supplements are best added at the time of bed preparation, described in step 5 in this chapter. (In appendix C, I give a list of the nutrient strengths of most commonly used organic soil supplements, as well as places to obtain them.)

2. Prepare the ground.

The best time to do this is in the fall. Begin by defining, with stakes and string, the outline of each bed. They can be as long as you want and should be no more than 3 to 4 feet wide so that you can easily reach the middle from either side to hoe, weed, harvest, and so forth. Try to keep the edges neat and straight.

Sink a stake at each corner of where you want the bed to be, then run a string from stake to stake to outline it. Leave a path 1 foot wide or so between the beds.

Now do a rough dig of each bed to the depth of your spade. First dig a trench across one end of the bed. This trench should be about 2 feet across, one "spit" (the depth of the blade of your spade) deep, and should run the full width of the bed, 3 to 4 feet. Take the soil you remove from this first trench and transport it to the other end of the bed. (This is the only time you will need to do this. The soil from the next trench you dig will be used to fill in the first one, and so on, until you arrive at the other end of the bed, when you will then use the dirt transported from the first trench to fill in the final one.)

Add 2 to 3 inches of manure to the bottom of the trench.

Now dig the second trench, right next to the first one. As you do, throw each spit of dirt from the second trench into the first one, filling it completely and then some. When the

Opening the first trench

Side view of trench

Skimming

second trench is completely dug out, the first one will be filled with rough clods and clumps of earth. Notice that since you've also mixed quite a bit of air into the soil in the process, as well as adding manure to the bottom of the trench, the surface of the first trench is now higher than it was before you started. This will be true of the entire bed when you're done.

If you're just beginning to garden, work for only two to three hours a day, as often as it suits you. Don't bite off more than you can chew. If your soil is already good and humusy, the digging will go faster and you'll cover a large area quickly. But if it's hard, compacted, and rocky, you'll go much slower and won't get as much done as soon. Even in this kind of soil, though, your pioneering work will pay off. When you go back in following years to redig these beds, you'll be surprised and gratified to find how much easier they are to work.

The object of the rough fall dig is to leave large clods and clumps of earth exposed to the elements. Loosened up like this, the soil is able to breathe and mellow under the cold-warm cycles of winter. Its miniature valleys catch moisture

Digging the second trench

Filling the first trench

and nutrients from the rain and snow that fall, and these then percolate downwards, soaking in deeply, helping prepare the bed for spring.

If there is grass on the site, skim it off with your spade (one good reason to have a square-ended spade) before you start digging, taking an inch or so of soil with it so that you get the growth portion near the top of the roots. Then either bury this sod in the bottom of the trench, along with the manure, or pile it up into a turf-loam compost, as I describe in the next step, below.

As you dig each new trench, throw ½ inch or so of manure across the slope that forms along the leading edge of the freshly dug part of the bed. (Slightly reduce the amount of manure you add to the bottom of each new trench if you are also putting skimmed-off sod there.) Over the winter, the sod, manure, and other organic materials will decompose and blend together, releasing warm, moist gases that help stimulate and nourish soil organisms.

If your soil is exceptionally hard to work, soak it first with the hose until it is thoroughly moist and then let it dry out enough so that it does not stick to your boots or your spade. If it's still very compacted, or full of rocks, break it up as much as possible, add some manure and work that in as well as you can, then sow a deep-rooting cover crop, like fava beans, alfalfa, or clover, or let weeds grow there to help break it up further. In the spring when you do a second dig to prepare for planting, you'll turn all this winter cover crop under as a rich green manure.

Although generally "the wisest way is rather to rejoice in and improve the soil fate has planted us on," as William Robinson was fond of saying, there are times when the soil simply isn't suitable and an alternative must be found. One of these is to simply lay a low wall or edging of railroad ties, large stones, or concrete block all around the site and then *add* a foot or so of good topsoil in the aboveground space you've just created. If you don't have suitable room in a backyard for regular beds, you might also consider gardening in containers. I grow a lot of my alpines and herbs in various kinds of pots and boxes. (Container growing is discussed in more detail in chapter 11.)

There are some parts of the country where leaving the earth exposed after the rough fall dig is not a good idea. Generally, wherever there is good snow cover on the ground throughout much of the winter, with overcast skies and low temperatures, you won't need to worry. In other places, however, like much of the Sunbelt, you will have to judge your local climatic conditions carefully to avoid overexposing newly turned soil to hot sun and strong winds, which can parch it and rob it of its precious nutrients and organic matter. In these locations I advise doing the rough fall dig, raking the beds smooth, and then adding a measure of additional protection, either by sowing a cover crop in early fall or laying down a thick mulch of leaves or compost on top of the beds.

3. Make fall compost.

There are four basic kinds of compost, and fall is a good time to prepare three of them: turf loam, leaf mold, and aged manure. The fourth, known as green or vegetable compost, is best made in the spring and is described in step 6, below.

Compost piles of any kind should be located in a partly shaded spot, such as near the east or north side of a building, away from tree roots. Before beginning to form the pile itself, you must first prepare the ground that it is to sit on. First skim off any surface growth until the earth is bare. (If this is sod, save it for the turf loam compost pile.) Don't remove too much topsoil — just enough (an inch or so) to keep grasses from growing back. Next break up the soil into large clods so that air, water, and soil organisms can pass back and forth between the ground and the pile itself, to aid in the processes of decomposition.

Turf loam. Turf loam is made from sod or "herbal ley," which is simply a general name for any mixture of grasses, weeds, and wildflowers, such as you might find in a pasture or meadow. Anytime you skim the grassy top layer off a patch of lawn to start a garden, you've got the makings of a turf loam compost pile in your spade. Turf loam is considered by many to be the king of composts, because it provides a fine, rooty, fibrous mixture of ingredients that is so rich in gentle nutrients it's like mother's milk for young plants. For this reason, turf loam is one of the main components used in making the soil mix that goes into seed flats, as I explain in chapter 11.

Making a turf-loam compost pile calls for some precision. First, begin by skimming off the sod or ley in even, rectangular slabs, all about the same length and width as the blade of your spade and an inch or so in thickness. Move these to the site you've chosen and prepared for your compost pile(s), and begin laying them in layers, one slab thick, like tiling a floor.

Lay the first layer with the sod side down, so that its growth surface is in direct contact with the turned and broken soil. Reverse the next layer, setting it sod side up, so that its soil surface is in contact with the soil surface of the first layer. Continue in this alternating fashion so that sod is always in contact with sod, soil with soil. Slope the sides of the pile inward slightly as you build. Stop when the pile is about 3 to 5 feet high, and cover it with a thin layer of dirt, straw, or grass clippings.

Leaf mold. Leaf-mold compost is nothing more than deciduous leaves, preferably oak or beech, raked into a pile and allowed to sit for a while. It is ideal for use in seed flats and around woodland plants like ferns and primulas — whenever a light, acidic, fibrous soil is called for. Make this pile as large as you can, because rain, snow, and decomposition will cause it to shrink by 60 percent or more. Also, step on the pile now and then while you're making it to crush the leaves and help encourage the process of decomposition. I let my kids jump in it while we're making it.

Aged manure. Unless you're lucky enough to live near a stable or dairy, this is a type of compost you will not be able to obtain quite as easily as turf loam or leaf mold. Most of it will have to be brought in from somewhere else, and most of what you acquire the first year will go straight into your beds, but I recommend getting enough so that some extra can be saved for use as a top dressing six months to a year later, when it has become very gentle indeed. (Never use fresh manure on your plants; always be sure it has been sitting for at least six months.)

For a backyard garden bed that is 4 feet by 40 feet (or two beds that are each 4 feet by 20 feet), you'll need about 2 cubic yards of manure. (A cubic yard is a pile 3 feet by 3 feet by 3 feet, and is about equal to four full wheelbarrows.) That will be enough to put 3 inches in the bottom of the trench right away and 1½ inches or more as a top dressing later.

The manure compost pile is as easy to make as the leaf-mold pile. Just form whatever manure you don't use in the fall rough dig this first year into a heap and let it sit. If you happen to have some clean straw available as well, mix in a little to help the air circulate. (Don't use hay, which has lots of seed in it, or the pile will sprout like crazy.)

Compost piles of any kind should be kept slightly moist — not soggy, just moist. You can check yours now and then by opening them up with a spade and reaching in to take a handful of material from the middle. It should feel humid, maybe a little damp, but should not drip when you squeeze it. If it seems somewhat too dry, water the entire pile gently, and let the water soak in. If it's too wet, you may need to turn the entire pile with your spade or fork to keep the necessary aerobic bacteria in it alive and active. You can also lay an old piece of carpet or a tarp on top of it to keep rain and snow from drenching it and washing out the nutrients, if you live in an especially rainy location.

Once you finish making a pile, "close" it by writing the date on a stake and planting it in or near the pile. Then leave it alone, except for testing and turning, if needed, until it is ready for use and can be opened.

Compost piles are ready to use when you can no longer distinguish the separate ingredients that went into making them — when leaves are no longer discernible as leaves, sod is no longer composed of soil and grass, and so forth. A finished compost pile should also not smell when opened, or steam, or feel hot to the touch. (Just warm is OK, though.) What it should do is yield the finest, richest, most humusy soil imaginable.

With no turning at all, nature alone will create a leaf mold ready for use in six months to a year, a well-aged manure in six months, and a turf loam (which should never be turned in any case) in one year.

If you have moisture problems, detect a foul smell emanating from the pile, or just want to speed up the composting process, you can turn the pile as often as every other week. This is also a good way to deal with the white fungus that sometimes develops on compost piles.

4. *Plan the garden.*

By now, your tools are in their places, clean, sharp, and ready. The ground is broken and mellowing into a rich, workable culture under winter's rain and snow. The turf-loam, leaf-mold, and manure piles are alive with microscopic life. The groundwork is done. Now it's time to take a break, relax your back, and release your imagination.

This is the time when you plan the garden itself, when you decide which rose, which French bean will go where, how to lead a path around a corner into the half-shade where violets will flourish. Now is the time to look forward to the red accent of a cardinal in the dogwood blossoms, the fresh-picked tomato that really does taste better than anything you can buy in the store.

Loosely sketch your plan on paper. This brings discipline to your reveries and helps you visualize the changes that will take place as your plants take root, grow into maturity, bring forth their fruit and blossoms, then wither and die to make room for something else. (Remember to plan for successive plantings as different crops come into season.)

As you plan, remember the needs of the seeds and growing plants, described in chapter 9. Remember that vegetables and sun-loving flowers need at least six hours of sunlight a day, and eight is better. Bear in mind that the

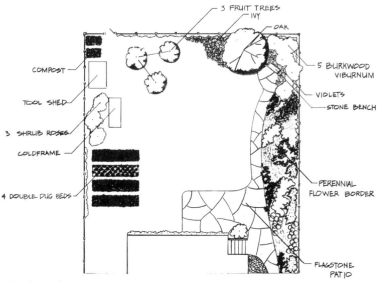

Garden plan

simple presence of a tree, fence, or body of water can make a dramatic difference in the microclimate of your garden. Don't forget that its low points will tend to be colder than its high points. Think about such details as the paths that people and animals tend to take when they cross your property. Keep in mind the fact that the edges of your beds will dry out faster than their middles, so those are the places to put plants that can tolerate drier conditions. Naturally, the more experience you get, the easier it is to do all this, but in the meantime you can gain much of the needed information from catalogues, nurseries, garden stores, and those neighborhood maestros.

If you're planning to grow vegetables, I recommend sticking to varieties you know you like already. Try a few unusual things if you want, but in general stay with those you know will be welcome on your table. I also believe in growing some flowers and herbs, even in gardens devoted primarily to vegetables. There are a number of good reasons for this.

First, some flowers, like pyrethrum and nicotiana, are natural insect controllers and will help protect your plants. Also, a diversity of plants is not the grand insect banquet that a monocrop is.

Cut flowers also make a good gift, one that is both personal and inexpensive. Herbs also serve this purpose admirably.

The main reason, though, has to do with what flowers attract, rather than what they repel: they will help lure *you* into the garden, and the more time you spend there, observing and enjoying it, the better it will do. I guarantee it. You'll notice problems in the making and nip them in the bud. You'll see which plants attract pests and which don't, which need more water and which are doing just fine. So, in making your plan, be sure to include some flowers and herbs.

As I say, the best planning aid you can possibly get is the advice of experienced gardeners in your neighborhood. Another good source is garden books and catalogues. I've listed those I particularly like in appendix A. Talking with other gardeners and browsing through these publications is a pleasant winter task.

As you plan, remember to be patient. You'll never be able to accomplish all that you can envision in the first year. Making a good garden takes time.

As spring approaches, your plan should be close enough to its final version so that you can think about visiting local garden stores and nurseries to see what they have to offer. I like to try and order from local sources as much as I can, but appendix A also gives some of the best national specialty firms for plants that simply may not be available in your area.

5. *Plant the garden.*

When spring finally comes and you are able to work outside, you'll find that your rough fall dig has made the job of preparing the beds for planting much easier. As soon as the soil is dry enough to work, you can begin to get beds ready for the hardier crops, like lettuce, peas, and radishes. Although you may still have some freezing nights and cool days ahead, these plants won't mind, and you'll have early salads for the table.

Tender crops like tomatoes and melons are susceptible to frost, however, and must not be put in the ground until all danger of it is past. If you push the season and plant these things too soon, they may flourish briefly only to be cut down by a late cold snap. It's OK to plant cold-weather crops a bit late in the season, but it's definitely risky to try to put tender things in the ground too soon.

Preparation of spring beds is very similar to the fall rough dig, but this time around you go deeper, using your fork on the lower levels. Begin as you did before, at one end of the bed. Dig the same sort of trench across its width, again making it 2 feet by 3 to 4 feet, and one spit deep. Again move the soil you take out of this first trench to the far end of the bed, to be used for filling in the final trench you dig.

Now, before you add manure to the bottom and slope of the trench, sink your fork into the floor of the bed, as deep as you can, to the full length of the tines if possible. Work the fork back and forth until cracks appear in the earth. Don't lift this soil up or turn it over; just loosen and crack it. Repeat this procedure over the entire floor of each trench,

Fork loosening the floor of the trench

taking care not to stand on the places you've loosened, as much as you can.

Now add manure, an inch or so, to the floor of the trench, and a thin layer, ½ inch or so, sprinkled across the slope at the leading edge of the freshly dug part as well. Continue in this way, filling each trench with soil from the new one next to it, until the entire bed has been double-dug and laced with aged manure.

As you work, remove large stones, buried debris like plastic or glass (I once unearthed an old set of bed springs in a garden I was digging for the first time), and large clumps of grass and weed roots — anything that may interfere with healthy, easy-to-work soil. I usually keep a bucket handy to toss this stuff in.

When you finish a bed, sprinkle a fine dusting of bone

meal and manure on the top. Then work this into the top few inches of the bed, and shape its surface with a fork or rake into a smooth, flat arc. Break up the larger clods of soil as you do, and pull out any more weeds, roots, or rocks that come to the surface. Once this is done, the bed is ready for planting.

You can start your garden from seed, of course, sowing it directly into the bed. In some cases — with carrots, radishes, and parsnips, for example — this is the only thing you can do because they should not be transplanted. These plants develop one strong central taproot (which is what we eat), and this makes transplanting them quite risky, since you may damage this root. In other cases, you can purchase many plants that have already been started for you at the local nursery or garden store and transplant them directly

Raking the bed smooth

into the bed. (See chapter 11 for more on starting and transplanting seeds.)

As I explained in chapter 9, it's very helpful to know your seed, to understand its native strengths. I like to shake a bit into my hand and hold it lightly in my open palm, while thinking about the mountain slope, open prairie, or cool woodland that it came from, imagining how its wild cousins — seeds blown in by winter winds, dropped into the natural leaf mold by birds, or carried in the fur of a hunting animal — are germinating there now.

I broadcast seed evenly to cover the whole bed, rather than planting it in rows. I want to use all the space that I've prepared. Row planting, to my mind, wastes it. Broadcasting causes the plants to come up densely, and a microclimate forms under their young leaves that moderates soil temperature, conserves moisture, and encourages mutual, beneficial growth among them all.

When you're ready to sow, pour some seed from the packet into your hand. Start by lightly shaking your whole arm, firmly, easily, slowly. Begin moving your arm back and forth over the near side of the bed. Sow in a continuous, even movement. Now go to the other side of the bed, and sow it in the same way.

The seed should fall like gentle rain. Not bouncing like hailstones, just falling softly, directly onto the bed. Allow more seed to fall on the edges, less as you move toward the middle. The edge is the difficult area because there is more drying and washing out, more wind and change there. The center has comparatively even conditions of moisture and warmth, and a higher percentage of seed will germinate there.

After sowing, lightly cover the seed with a fine compost or your best *sifted* garden soil. The rule is to cover the seed to a depth that is twice its own thickness, but don't worry overly about taking this rule too literally — just sprinkle on compost (or topsoil) until the seed just barely disappears. Another way to cover seed, faster but less exact, is to gently rake over the bed after sowing, to mix soil and seed. Finally, lightly press the covering soil down all over the freshly sown area with your hand or the back of a rake, to bring the seed into close contact with soil moisture.

6. *Make spring compost.*

Spring is the busy time in gardening, the time when you have everything going for you. The weather calls you outdoors. The lengthening days invite plants to reach upward. The gradual warming of the soil draws the seed into germination and growth. Gentle rains refresh the garden and the gardener.

As your shoots come up and trees leaf out again, so do the weeds. This young green growth is especially desirable for spring compost-making, mainly because of its high nitrogen content. As a plant ages, the percentage of nitrogen in it decreases and the proportion of carbon increases. It gets woodier and harder, which means that it decomposes more slowly in the compost pile.

I usually spend one whole day or so in the late spring season making green compost. Taking my secateurs or hedge clippers, or even a scythe, I go to an open field or empty lot and chop down lots of fresh young vegetation, for free. (I make sure not to use weeds or grass clipping that have been treated with an herbicide in any of my compost piles.) I prefer weeds because they not only contain a rich mixture of nutrients and minerals, but also embody a kind of wild vigor that I like to maintain in my garden. Some weeds, such as mustards, are beneficial in other ways as well, because they secrete alkaline substances that can help sweeten an overly acid soil.

To make the spring compost pile itself, prepare the ground as I explained in step 3. Skim off the sod and break the exposed earth up roughly. Make sure the location is in a partly shady spot, away from large trees.

When the site is ready, put down a 3-inch layer of small branch clippings or tough, carbonaceous old stems directly on the ground. Sunflower and Jerusalem artichoke stalks are particularly well suited for this purpose. Crisscross them so they function something like a fire grate, letting air flow under and up into the pile. This nourishes the aerobic microbes that do the work of decomposition.

Next add a 12- to 18-inch layer of all the green growth you've just collected. You can mix in grass clippings from the lawn if you like, but don't let them bunch up into matted clumps because then they won't decompose properly.

On top of that layer you can add organic kitchen scraps — old lettuce leaves, rotten tomatoes, potato and carrot peelings, sour milk (an especially good compost additive), and so forth. Since you want to have a fair amount of this material already available when you make the green compost pile, it's smart to start saving it some weeks beforehand. A standard plastic garbage can with a tight lid, placed outside the back door, makes an excellent temporary holding tank. Anything that will decompose can be added to this layer, but avoid plastics, color-printed papers, cigarette butts, and, if animals are a problem, meat and bones.

Finally, add a 1-inch layer of topsoil to the pile, over everything else. Repeat the green matter/kitchen scraps/topsoil sequence four or five more times, until the pile is 4 to 6 feet high. Remember to slope the sides just slightly inward toward the top, and to cover the whole pile with a thin layer of topsoil, aged manure, or mulch when it's done. Close it, and plant your date label nearby. Moisten it thoroughly. With no turning, this compost will be ready for use in two to three months, or less in hot weather. It should be used within one year.

The All-in-One Pile. If you don't have the time, inclination, or space to make four separate compost piles, you can make just one, in which green matter, leaf mold, turf loam, and manure are combined. You won't be able to supplement your beds as precisely as you can with four different piles, but this approach is simpler and more convenient.

Follow the directions given above for making the spring green compost pile, but when you get to the second layer — weeds, grass clippings, and such — add in some leaves and manure also. Instead of topsoil, in the fourth layer, used skimmed-off sod, placed with the sod side down, but chop up the slabs first. Don't put them in whole as you would for a turf-loam compost. And use manure, straw, or topsoil as a final covering over the whole, finished pile; avoid sod here because it may take root and grow. One other good substance to toss into the all-in-one pile is a sprinkling of wood ash.

7. Cultivate the garden.

By early summer your garden will have taken on a life of its own. Crocus and scillas will have come and gone. The spring peas will be delicious, the roses in bud. The strawberries will be blooming, and the first small fruit will be forming under their leaves.

If you've prepared well, the garden will almost take care of itself at this stage, and you will be able to step back and guide it into its midsummer crescendo. The role to play

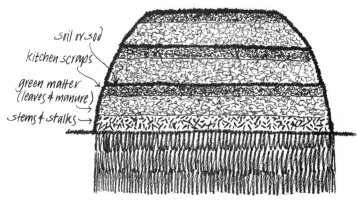

soil or sod
kitchen scraps
green matter
(leaves & manure)
stems & stalks →

Compost

now is that of faithful attendant, providing whatever is needed for the garden's continued health, eliminating whatever may cause disease or other problems.

As the summer moves on, the light rains of spring are usually left behind, and it becomes more important for you to replace them. Water regularly, from above. Listen to the water hitting the bed (or plants), and make the sound as quiet as possible to avoid disturbing the soil or damaging the crops. Water in a sweeping arc in one area until a glistening shine appears on the surface of the soil, then move on to another spot. Return to each watered place two or three times, moving the hose when that shiny surface appears. As you water, keep an eye out for plants that are regularly wilting by early morning or that stay wilted into the late afternoon hours, and give them extra moisture if the soil around them is dry. (But remember that wilting is a sign of trouble only under these conditions; in the full heat of the day it's usually a natural defense system.)

Until the leaves of your plants are big enough to fully shade the surface of the beds, hoe around them lightly once a week or so to break up the crust that forms on the soil.

Left unbroken, it can form a strangling collar around the stem of a plant and check its growth. Shallow hoeing keeps this from happening and opens up the surface of the bed, allowing for the free movement of air and water past its surface.

You'll only need to do this for a few weeks, until the surface of your beds disappears under a leafy green canopy, which serves to keep the soil cool and loose and moist. (Slip your hand under this canopy on a hot summer afternoon and you'll feel how much lower the temperature is there than in the places that are exposed to direct sun.)

Weeds will proliferate vigorously now. When they first appear, welcome them as a temporary soil umbrella and because their deep-mining roots help open up the beds at lower depths. Thin them just enough to keep them from shading out the growth of your own crops, turning them lightly back into the top layer of the soil with a trowel or hoe, or removing them completely and adding them to the green compost pile. When your plants are big enough to take over this function for themselves, remove most of the remaining weeds, leaving just a few — wild sunflower, lamb's quarter — for the birds. As I explain in step 9, it's a good idea to do all you can to invite birds into the garden, not only for their beauty and their song, but because they are a first line of defense against insect predators.

Newly planted tomatoes and green peppers will benefit from a paper collar about now to protect them against cutworms, a pest that likes to topple them bodily. Use a toilet paper core, cut in half, or a Dixie cup with the bottom cut out, and just push it partway into the soil around the stem of each plant while it is still small.

Now is also the time to start removing damaged or diseased leaves and branches, to help keep infection and bugs

Cutworm collar

at bay. Any plants that are seriously diseased or dead should be removed completely and thrown out.

Plants that need staking (e.g., delphiniums, hollyhocks) or support of another kind, such as trellises for beans or cages for tomatoes, should get it now, while they're still young. Trellis posts should be set even earlier, before the plants are in the ground; you risk damaging the roots if you wait until they're already settled in their beds.

As you harvest spring crops (see step 10, below), begin to prepare your summer succession plantings — the beans, corn, squash, or summer annual flowers that will follow the early, cool-season peas, beets, and radishes. A good gardener's tip for spring is to make your plants grow quickly and harvest them young, while leaves are tender, radishes are mild (the longer you leave them in the ground the hotter they get), and rhubarb stems are tart but not woody.

8. *Observe the garden.*

By June, peonies, roses, and lupines are in bloom. Herbs are fully leaved out and ready for use. Your schedule of

165

hoeing, watering, and gleaning the fruits of your labor should be well established by now.

This is the time to again step back, observe, and learn. Return now and then to that same chair from which you surveyed the possibilities of your site, back in chapter 9. Take another look, making use of camera and sketch pad if you wish. Note the flower combinations that work especially well together; one of my favorites is pale blue delphinium and common yellow coreopsis. Record the varieties of vegetables that are thriving, for next year's seed order. Jot down how much your favorite lettuce bed produced. Was the flavor of that tarragon all you had hoped for? Which plants besides the carrots didn't come up at all? (New gardeners often find carrots hard to grow for a number of reasons: The seed is tiny and easily washed out of the bed, so water *very* gently for the first three weeks or so. The bed has to be kept moist, or the seeds will dry out. Also, carrots take a relatively long time to germinate — twenty-one days or more.)

Nature herself is full of vigor at this season, and it's a good time for walks in the fields and woods, for noticing the similarities between domesticated plants and their wild cousins, between carrot and Queen Anne's lace, spinach and lamb's quarter, garden and wild iris. Discovering a healthy wild lettuce and observing its station — moist, half-shaded, at the edge of the woods — can lead you to plant next year's summer crop differently, say in leafier soil in the half-shade of a bean trellis, to keep it from drooping and going bitter in the full sun.

9. *Control pests.*

By midsummer, tomatoes and beans are ripening, penstemons are in flower, and seed formation is going on all

Wild rose and native dianthus

around. The year is moving onward. From its peak at the summer solstice, the daylength is starting to decline, to turn toward winter and the end of summer's expansiveness. Now, when pests can become a problem, is the time to focus on appropriate control measures.

The first and most effective of these is simple prevention. *Grow healthy plants.* Like humans, plants are naturally more resistant to disease and insects when they are strong and healthy. In my fifteen years of gardening, I have had almost no serious problems with insects or disease, mainly because the methods I follow do grow healthy crops.

What makes a plant healthy? Deep beds, chock-full of organic matter, providing plenty of rootrun, an even soil temperature, consistent moisture, and a sustained, gradual supply of nutrients. A vital, balanced community of soil microbes, insects, birds, and other organisms that can meet surges in pest populations with corresponding increases in their natural enemies. Good sunlight. And, above all, an attentive gardener, who can detect serious problems in the making and stop them before they get out of hand, but who also knows that there must be a place in the garden for slugs, bacteria, and life's end.

Remedies for slug and snail excesses are legion. Beer in sunken pans, salt applied directly to them, a heavy foot, rings of sharp grit or wood ash around the base of each plant — all these and more have been tried and found to be of use by some gardeners. You will have to experiment a bit to find the method that works for you. I just pick up slugs or snails and eject the intruder bodily from the premises as I make my early morning garden rounds. More often than not, I find this approach works well for the larger insect pests also, though it is admittedly more time-consuming than spraying. Remember that since these creatures tend to feed at night and hide during the heat of the day, it's best to go hunting very early in the morning. When you find one — caterpillar, tomato worm, slug, or snail — just pluck it from the leaf, step on it, toss it far away, or feed it to the chickens.

Wild birds and domestic ducks, geese, and chickens are probably the best friends you could have in helping keep your crops free of insect predators. Do everything in your power to make them welcome. They may exact a small toll in seeds, buds, shoots, and soft fruits, but the price is almost always well worth it. Do also, however, put netting over your berry plants and tie black thread from the branches of fruit trees (birds don't see the string until they fly into it, and this annoys them enough to make them avoid these trees) that you want them to stay out of.

If you find your insect problems do become severe enough to call for more drastic measures, insecticides are a last resort. Confer with your county extension agent or other reliable local sources and select the substance that is *most specific* to the problem and *least persistent* in the environment.

Give first consideration, when appropriate, to the organic pesticides: pyrethrum, rotenone, and nicotine (see appendix D for suppliers). Natural pesticides can be highly effective. For example, pyrethrum, a kind of chrysanthemum, provides an excellent countermeasure for aphids and caterpillars, among other pests. And it is harmless to humans. Natural pesticides have some distinct advantages over artificials. Pyrethrum, for example, has been used for hundreds of years without causing resistance in insects exposed to it.

Like any other life form, plants can also get diseases. Viral infections, caused by submicroscopic life forms that we still know relatively little about, show up in symptoms like strangely twisted and curled leaves and mottled leaf markings called "mosaics." Not all plant viruses are destructive, but your only recourse when your crops contract one that is harmful (your county extension agent can give you the diagnosis) is to remove and thoroughly dispose of the plants involved.

Bacterial and fungoid diseases can usually be handled more gently. Fungi such as those that cause powdery mildew do not like sunlight, dryness, and fresh air. When a fungus problem appears, remove the affected parts of the plant and arrange to give it drier, sunnier, airier conditions. Maybe water left on the leaves overnight is the culprit; try watering only in the mornings, or just watering less. Maybe it's overcrowding; try thinning around the plant. Maybe it's too much shade; try pruning out some of the branches overhead to open it up to the sun. An herbal preparation made from equisetum (horsetail) is also recommended as a preventive for fungus diseases by many biodynamic gardeners.

Sprays are available for most bacterial and fungoid problems, but here again these should be regarded as last-ditch options. The first thing to do is try altering the circumstances that allow these unwelcome visitors into the garden in the first place.

There are times when none of your changes, remedies, or sprays will work, and you will have to accept defeat, at least for the moment. A gardener is sometimes called upon to be ruthless, and intractable disease is one of those times. Remove the infected growth entirely and redig the beds, opening them up to the purifying influences of air and sunlight. Then plant them with a cleansing herb — yarrow, chamomile, or marigold — and wait for next spring's renewal.

10. Harvest.

With the passing of summer, the sun's arc begins to sink back toward the equator. The days get shorter and the angle of light more oblique. Winter is coming, contraction is in the land. Over many millennia, plants have learned to heed this message. And so they do everything they can to perpetuate their species: they make blossoms, fruit, and seeds, and store energy in tissue and root.

Harvesting, like some of the other steps described in this chapter, actually goes on intermittently throughout the spring and summer. But it reaches a kind of peak in late summer and early fall, and there are some simple rules to follow at these times.

Most fruits and vines (tomatoes, peaches, grapes, for instance) should be harvested at the end of the day because that is when their vitamin content is highest. Roots, stems, and leaves (turnips, rhubarb, and cabbage, for example) should instead be collected in the morning because that is when they are juiciest and most flavorful. Flowers should also be cut in the morning because that is when they are most fragrant and when, having taken in moisture all night, they will stand up longer in the vase. In my experience, herbs are best gathered in the later morning hours.

The quintessential harvest is the seed, the bridge to the next year's crops, and collecting it is a simple practice. Beginning in early spring, as soon as the first shoots appear in your garden, observe those that do best. Reserve them for your seed stock, and mark them with a ribbon.

When these plants flower, select a branch or flower, not the first or second to open but the third, fourth, or fifth — one of those toward the middle of the flowering cycle — and allow the fruit or seed to develop on it. With some plants, such as lettuce, cabbage, radishes, and broccoli, you will have to be concerned about cross-pollination from unwanted sources in your neighborhood, so cover these flowers with a paper bag. With self-pollinating plants, like tomatoes, beans, melons, and cucumbers, this is not a problem.

Let these seed-stock plants continue to mature fully, to the point where their fruit is beginning to dry out. Then either pull the entire plant out of the ground and hang it upside down in a cool, dry place, or take the fruit off the plant, clean the pulp from the seed, and lay it out to dry. Once it is dry, put the seed in an airtight bag or jar and store that in a cool, dry place. With plants like lettuce or hollyhock that form dry seed, merely shake the seed from the flowerhead into the bag or jar.

Seed harvested in this way will remain viable for at least a year, and often much longer. (A few herb seeds, such as angelica, or rock-garden-plant seeds, which are closer to their wild form, must be germinated fresh and cannot be stored for long.)

Finally, after all else, harvest for the compost pile. Take everything that's left in the garden and build a new fall heap, following the directions given above in step 6 for green compost. By cleaning the garden of old growth and composting it, you are preparing for the garden's continuity, for beginning the cycle anew.

Year 2: The Widening Cycle

*g*ardening gets easier the second year. Most of the pioneering work is behind you now. You can concentrate on simplifying and improving your practice.

Fall Again

In the second year, your homegrown compost will largely replace the aged manure you were buying to fertilize and enhance your soil. This has at least two happy results. First, properly composted organic matter — whether it's made of green leaves, manure, or a mixture of both — is a *controlled* garden process. It conserves nutrients and humus and has a special soil life.

Most freely available stable and feedlot manure, how-ever — invaluable as it is for starting a garden — has not been well composted. It can, therefore, vary a good deal in quality. Some is superb, but much will have been so ex-posed to the elements that it will have lost most of its nutri-tional value by the time it gets to your garden. And barnyard manure can sometimes develop high concentrations of mineral salts, which can steal water from plants and "burn" them in the process.

So, handy as manure is for the beginner, or for those rare gardeners who have access to a reliable, high-quality source, most of us find that compost is the preferable alternative once the garden is well under way. Compost does not develop high levels of sulphates, chlorides, and other potentially harmful salts. It is made up of a wider range of ingredients than manure is. And because compost is cultured, it does not lose nutrients to rain, snow, and sun as exposed manure does.

The second good thing about relying on compost instead of manure is that you can collect and grow it yourself. Unless you happen to have livestock, you aren't likely to have a source of manure nearby. Composting offers you a sound way of disposing of your own garden and kitchen wastes while building soil fertility.

At the beginning of this second year, you will have a fair amount of potential compost fuel on hand — those late summer beans, squash, cucumbers, and fall pea vines, as well as the leaves and stems of the annual flowers you've been cutting. All this can be harvested for composting, before the frost turns them brown. You may also be able to collect local weeds that are still green for compost, though they will be less abundant than they are in the spring. Such herbs as comfrey, valerian, and yarrow are another excellent compost ingredient. But be sure to just cut the tops off for the pile; leave the roots so these plants will come back again next year.

Some sections of your cultivated beds may still be producing late-season broccoli, spinach, parsnips, chrysanthemums, and such. In other areas clear out the late summer crops, compost them, redig the beds, or just lightly rake the surface for seed, and then sow new compost crops. White and crimson clover and hairy vetch, as well as winter rye and alfalfa are good choices.

Now that you have cultured beds, i.e., beds that have been double-dug and put through a full season of cultivation, you can afford to plant a number of crops that demand good soil and that will make your garden much easier to manage. In particular, I'm referring to hardy bulbs, perennial flowers and vegetables, and fruit plants, both trees and berries.

If you are on tight clay, you should redig the beds each fall and spring, adding compost until drainage is good. On sandy soil, working in compost will soon give them a fluffier texture. Once the soil texture is good, you can dig beds less often, perhaps once a year or biannually, and protect the soil from the sun, wind, and drought with mulch, cover crops, and, of course, garden plants.

I often redig the garden in fall because I thoroughly enjoy double-digging seasoned beds. They are so easy to work, compared to the first digging, and I get to see and feel the texture of the soil firsthand. Repeated double-digging continues to improve aeration and introduces compost deeply, which helps draw roots down. It also buries weed seeds so far below the surface they cannot germinate. But the digging must be done quickly and new plants started immediately to shade the ground.

So, before you begin any new fall planting, first decide whether you want to redig your beds. Also decide whether you want to make your garden larger. If you do, now is the time to rough-dig any new footage, sow a cover crop, and let winter help soften up the earth for you. (See the instructions on rough-digging under step 2 in chapter 10.)

Before we go on, I recommend getting a few new tools.

For seed raising and transplanting, you will need a small, three-pronged hand fork and a riddle, which is a sieve with quarter-inch wire mesh for sifting the soil mix used in seed flats. You will also need to purchase a small amount of lumber and related materials for making cold frames and seed flats. These materials are described in more detail below.

Fall is the right time to put out perennial flowers (like peonies, campanula, and coralbells) and the hardy bulbs (narcissus, crocus, scilla, lilies and so on). When planting bulbs, remember that they need good drainage.

Choose a place that does not get soggy. Dig a hole (or trench, if you want to plant a bunch of bulbs in a "drift") to a depth that is four times the diameter of the bulb. Add sand to the bottom for drainage, mix it well with the loose soil there, drop in a sprinkling of bone meal for each bulb (they're phosphorus lovers), add the bulb(s), and cover. (Make sure the pointed end is upward.) You'll know spring is coming when you see their strong green spears forcing their way up through the earth into the light and warmth.

Perennial Vegetables. Only two common vegetables are hardy perennials: asparagus and rhubarb. A third, less common but good perennial vegetable is Jerusalem artichoke. Once planted, these will return to growth each year on their own, a fact that simplifies the gardener's life considerably.

Asparagus is the king of homegrown vegetables, and as such deserves special preparations. In a bed, dig two trenches 2 feet apart down its length. If you are planting just a few asparagus, the trenches will be shorter. Since asparagus roots are wide-ranging, allow 3 feet between plants in each trench, and stagger them so that a plant in one trench is opposite the space between two plants in the neighboring trench. Now put 6 to 8 inches of compost or high-quality manure in the bottom of the hole. Add another 4 to 6 inches of the garden loam you just dug out of the trenches, or topsoil mixed with compost. For each plant, stir in a handful of bone meal and, if available, wood ash. Now, on 3-foot centers, set the asparagus "crown" — the roots and central stem — in the hole, which should be about 1 foot deep by this time. Spread the roots out gently so the crown looks like a resting octopus. Cover with 4 inches of good garden soil, leaving a 6- to 8-inch depression. As the asparagus spears grow and rise through the soil, gradually fill in this depression with more good, humusy material.

All of this careful preparation makes a fine, nutrient-rich, moisture-retentive rootrun for these special plants. Burying them so deeply ensures that their roots, which are easily damaged by the hoe, are well protected. Prepared in this way and regularly nourished, an asparagus plant will begin to produce harvestable spears in two years, and continue to do so for half a century or more.

Putting rhubarb out is simpler. Dig a hole to a depth of only a foot or so. Mix compost or aged manure into the earth at the bottom of the hole. Set the roots in the hole, and fill with good soil. The crown should be set at soil level. Plant them about 2½ to 3 feet apart.

Rhubarb is vigorous: add compost or some other organic

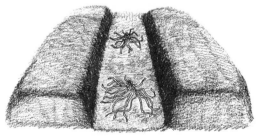

Asparagus planting

mulch every year, water regularly, and you should be able to eat rhubarb pie every spring for the rest of your life. Be sure to eat only the stems and avoid the leaves, which have heavy concentrations of toxic oxalic acid. Also, don't eat rhubarb raw.

Many herbs are perennial. Sage, thyme, lemon balm for tea, chives, garlic, horseradish, lovage, a couple of different mints, oregano, sorrel are a few of the valuable kitchen herbs. French tarragon is wonderful in salad, with green beans, or with fish and is seldom found in stores.

Planting perennial herbs is simpler yet. With the exception of lovage, all of them like full sun. Except for the mints, which will run on you and need to be kept in an odd corner, I find that the ends of my beds, right along the central path, are ideal places for herbs. They're handy here, ready to be picked for the pot or given to friends.

One caution: In herbs, nitrogen's tendency to promote quick leaf growth also has the effect of reducing their concentration of essential oils, which is what gives them their fragrance and distinctive taste. So avoid using fertilizers with a medium to high nitrogen content in and around your herbs. I find that compost serves me perfectly well for this purpose.

Fruit. The queen of all perennial crops, one that demands a deep, rich, humusy bed, is fruit, both soft fruit (berries) and tree fruit. (Fruit plants can be safely planted in the fall in the eastern states and parts of the Pacific Coast, but in most of the West, because of our erratic winters, I wait until spring.)

All bramble fruits, from raspberries and blackberries to gooseberries, like humusy, well-cultivated beds. The soil should be slightly acid, and if you have any doubt about the pH, mix in some oak-leaf mold, which is acidic. Open sunlight, with some protection from heavy winds, is also desired by these fruits, as well as plenty of moisture and good drainage.

On a year-old bed, dig a hole twice as large as the roots, make a small mound of soil in the bottom of the hole (like a cone), spread the roots out over this mound, and half-fill the hole with good loamy soil. Now work the soil around the roots with your fingers, just like Olmsted planting a tree, to make sure there are no air pockets and the roots are in good contact with the soil. Finish filling the hole, and soak deeply. Most berry plants are easy to grow and very vigorous.

To keep the "canes" from flopping over and rooting everywhere, tie them to a trellis or within wires fastened to corner poles. Dig up roots that get out of their area of the bed. For raspberries, after harvest cut out all the canes that fruited that summer, and thin new ones to five to eight per plant. In the spring, prune back these new canes to about 4½ feet in height to force them to send out lateral shoots, which will maximize their harvest. Because birds love berries, you may need to throw a light netting over them at fruiting time, in the summer.

A fruit tree is a long-term project and deserves a good start. Dig a big hole, then make it bigger, big enough to accommodate the spread-out roots, perhaps 2 feet wide by 18 inches deep for a mail-order tree. Mix compost into the soil that you plan to backfill the hole with. Add a few handfuls of bonemeal, and toss a few old nails or a tin can into the hole for added minerals. If your compost doesn't already have wood ash in it, add a handful of this nutrient too.

The nursery will probably include directions for pruning the trees it sends. In general, at planting time prune back the main stem and side branches, from the top down, by one-half to one-third of their length. This forces the stem to send forth new branches around the trunk at a low level, making the strong "scaffold" you want for abundant leaf and fruit growth. Ideally, a dwarf fruit tree's branches should fan out from the central stem, or "leader," at 4- to 8-inch intervals and should be located around the leader as they rise, something like a spiral staircase.

Place the tree in the hole, spread its roots out carefully (remove any burlap or wire that may be holding the root ball intact), and fill with good soil and compost. If the tree is grafted — that is, has one kind of root stock and a different kind of top, or scion — don't plant the graft below ground level or the scion will form its own roots. (The graft will be visible as a bump or crook in the trunk, near the base of the tree.)

I prefer to plant fruit trees that are only one year old, known as "maidens." This means waiting a year or two longer to get fruit from them, but I think it's worth it in terms of long-term health. A tree becomes less tolerant of changes once it has become established in the nursery. Its north side has acquired a tolerance to cool winds, and its south side has gotten used to intense sun and greater shifts in temperature. Uprooted and sent to a gardener like you or me, it isn't likely to wind up with the same north-south orientation, and readapting is hard on it. Also, the more time you give a fruit tree to develop strong roots before it comes into bearing, the better.

Most new trees need to be staked, and this should be done when they are planted so their roots aren't injured later. Secure the tree to the stake with material that is both broad and elastic — wide rubber bands, wide garden tape, strips of old carpet. Don't use wire or hard cord. It will cut into the bark and girdle the tree, inviting disease and death.

Water a freshly planted tree immediately after planting and then regularly throughout its first growing season. A newly planted tree should grow 2 to 3 feet in its first year. If it doesn't, increase the supply of water or fertilizer or both.

Berries should produce fruit within a year. Dwarf fruit trees will come into bearing in three to six years, depending on the variety. Peaches are the earliest, with flowers and fruit in three years or sooner; plums come into bearing in three to four years; and pears and most apples, a year or two after that. And all will continue to bear for decades thereafter.

Extending the Season. If you happen to live in an area with long, mild falls and early springs, you're lucky. You can follow your summer beans, melons, and annual flowers with another round of cool-season spinach, broccoli, Swiss chard, carrots, lettuce, Chinese cabbage, and mums and get three gardens a year — spring, summer, and fall — with no special effort at all. And you'll find, moreover, that many of your fall crops do even better when there's a nip in the air — it improves their flavor. Parsnips, rutabaga, and cabbage, for example, are especially responsive to Jack Frost's touch.

If you aren't so blessed, however, you'll have to work a little harder to extend your growing season. One simple way is to plant crops in fall that "overwinter" until the following spring. This means that the seeds of plants like spinach and leek will, if planted in the fall, germinate, send forth roots and leaves, and begin to grow. But then, when winter sets in, they go into a state of suspended animation, surviving quite nicely for months on end under a covering of snow or a deep pile of leaves. When spring returns, they wake up, none the worse for wear, and begin growing in the warming sunlight, maturing well ahead of plants not sown until then, when the soil is often still too cold for rapid germination.

Overwintering is also a good practice for some flowers, like sweet peas and calendulas, which detest hot summers. They will thank you for a fall sowing by blossoming in spring while the weather is still cool.

Cold frames. Another tried-and-true way to extend the growing season, both later into the fall and earlier in the spring, is by using a simple solar device known as a cold frame. A cold frame is nothing more than a wooden box, often measuring 3 feet in width and twice that in length, with no bottom and an open top covered with plastic or glass.

The purpose of a cold frame is simply to capture and hold the sun's warmth, like a miniature greenhouse. Plants that are still too young or too sensitive to face the rigors of outdoor living are placed inside it for a little extra protection from the cold. Plants started indoors, for example, are usually not ready for the higher levels of ultraviolet light and the low temperature outside. They need a transitional period of adjustment, of acclimation, of toughening up (known as "hardening-off"), and the cold frame is a good way to provide this for them.

Some cold frames are made to be portable and can be moved from place to place as needed. Others are permanent installations, and plants can either be sown directly in them or grown in seed flats and pots. The top of a cold frame is a clear panel you can either lift and remove or raise to let fresh air in and excess heat and humidity out. (Busy gardeners can buy automatic timers to do this for them while they're at work or out for the day.) Watering plants in a cold frame requires daily attention when they are actively growing.

Cold frames can be rudimentary. I have one made out of the frame of a child's bed, covered with plastic. I ventilate it by tilting the whole thing up on a rock or stick. Basic wooden ones are easy to make, and fall is a good time to do so. The simple one pictured below can be constructed for $40 or less in materials, and a day of labor.

The art of using glass, or more recently, plastic, to collect solar energy and thus speed up a plant's natural growth cycles (a process known as "forcing") has been part of gardening for centuries. It reached something of a peak in the hands of French market gardeners (*maraichers*) at the turn of the century, when acreages were covered with cold frames and "cloches" (a bell-shaped jar used for individual plants — the forerunner of today's "hotcap"). In those days, when Paris traveled by horse, copious quantities of manure

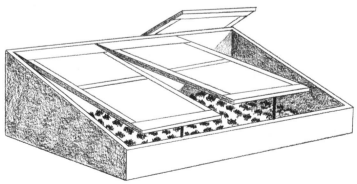

Cold frames

were laid in the ground under cold frames, thus making "hot beds" to force vegetables in winter and keep Parisians supplied with fresh produce.

Although glass still holds the aesthetic edge, the advantages of plastic's lighter weight and reduced breakability have made it the favored medium for cold frames and cloches today. (A basic cloche can be made by cutting off the bottom of a large plastic jug. You can remove the cap for ventilation. Push it firmly into the soil so it doesn't blow away.) If you want to start a few pepper or tomato plants early, plant them on a warm day and set the cloches over them. Thus protected, they can be well established weeks before your first frost-free date.

Seed flats. Hand in hand with the use of a cold frame goes the use of seed flats, and fall is a good time to make these invaluable garden implements as well. As the diagram below shows, they're not hard to construct.

I make my flats out of redwood "bender board." Because it stays dry, redwood (or cedar) helps prevent disease and

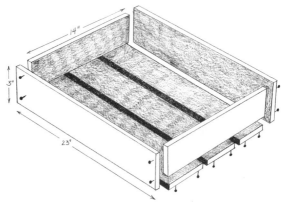

Seed-flat construction

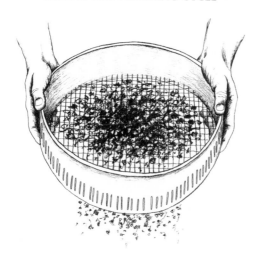

Riddle

insect problems, and bender board (used for lawn edging) is commonly available in lumberyards. Buy the thickest pieces you can find. Remember to leave a gap between the bottom slats for drainage.

I make my own soil mix for seed sowing. My recipe is the traditional one, but I should point out that commercial greenhouses now approach the whole matter of seed flats and mixes in a very different way than they did fifty years ago. First, they use disposable plastic trays, not wooden flats, and they fill them with sterile, soilless mixes. This is done because plastic trays are cheaper than wooden flats, and soilless mixes are inexpensive and lightweight and lend themselves to regular applications of synthetic fertilizers and pesticides. All very advantageous in today's nursery business, but also very wasteful (those plastic trays, made of petrochemicals, are thrown away after a season of use) and far too dependent on chemicals inimical to the microbial populations I strive to encourage in my beds.

The mix I make is known as "a third, a third, and a third,"

for the simple reason that it is made of one-third good garden soil, one-third "sharp" sand (i.e., sand that hasn't been worn smooth yet and feels gritty to the touch), and one-third leaf mold to provide added body and keep the mix from compacting as it is repeatedly watered. This is the mix that Alan recommended. (If you have turf loam, use it in place of the soil portion to give the seedlings' diet the quality of mother's milk.)

The mix is easy to make. Place your newly acquired riddle in the wheelbarrow, and shovel about one spadeful of each of the three main ingredients listed above into it, a little at a time. Each time you fill up the riddle, lift and shake it to strain out lumps of clay, stones, stems, and undecomposed leaves. Line the bottom of the flat with about ¼ inch of the strained-out twigs and leaves.

When you have a total of about twelve spadefuls in the wheelbarrow, all sifted through the riddle, blend the mix by lifting a spadeful at a time and letting it rain back down into the barrow. Keep doing this until everything is thoroughly mingled. Then try the squeeze test. The mix should feel springy and slightly gritty, and should hold its shape. Stockpile some of the mix where you can keep it moist and shaded for use in very early spring.

Here's how to prepare a seed flat: Put a thin layer of leaf mold into the bottom of the flat; young roots adore the stuff. If you have access to it, seaweed is a good supplement to add at this point. (Crumbly or powdered seaweed can also be added directly to the mix as you make it in the barrow.) Seaweed has a full assortment of nutritious trace elements and helps prevent fungus problems as well. Bracken fern is another soil-mix additive with desirable cleansing and tonic properties.

Fill the flat to overflowing with the mix, then level the top

Pressing the edges of a seed flat   Sowing a seed flat

off with your hand or a board. Now, just inside the side boards, press your fingertips vertically downward all around the circumference of the flat.

Fill in the compressed edges with more mix (don't compact this addition), then brush the surface level again with your hand.

The final step is to press the entire surface of the flat smooth, with either a small pressing board or a mason's wooden finishing trowel, to prepare it to take seed. Press down firmly but not too hard all across the flat. The mix should settle down to a uniformly even level about ½ inch below the top of the sides of the flat. Check the feel of the soil: it should bounce back slightly under the pressing board.

The Second Winter

Forget the garden. After a welcome respite, I find myself reverting to armchair gardening, browsing the catalogues, and then planning anew. (Appendix E describes some garden design ideas that make use of the methods of the great gardeners described in Part 2.)

Spring Returns

Early on, indoors or in the cold frame, sow some flats and you'll have seedlings ready to transplant into the beds as soon as they warm up.

Two general kinds of plants are especially suited to starting indoors in seed flats in the late winter or early spring. One is those that take a long time to germinate and are slow to grow once they do germinate. This group includes lilies, many herbaceous perennials, like chrysanthemums, and some herbs, such as sage and rosemary. These should be sown in midwinter.

The other group includes all the plants of early spring: lettuce, spinach, calendula, broccoli, parsley, and Swiss chard. Sown in a seed flat in late winter or early spring and placed on a warm windowsill or table top, they'll be ready for hardening-off in the cold frame and then transplanting into the garden soil as soon as it is workable. This can give you as much as a month's head start come spring.

I like to time my sowing to the monthly cycle of the moon. The moon's magnetic pull on the moisture in the earth increases twice monthly, with the new and full moon. So I make a practice of sowing slow germinators (perennials, generally) just before the full moon. Fast germinators (annuals, as a rule) go into my flats (or the beds, in spring) just before the new moon.

Before you sow any seed, write the name of its variety, where you got it, and the date sown on a plastic label. Then keep that label with those plants throughout their life, from seed flat to garden bed to harvest records. When you find the perfect squash, you'll remember what it's called, where to reorder it, when to plant it next year, and when to expect to be able to put it on the table again.

You sow a flat in much the same way that you sow a bed (see chapter 10). Pour plenty of seed from the packet into your hand. Without letting the seed fall, begin moving your hand in a slow circle over the outer edges of the flat. As you do this, imagine the seed falling, evenly spaced, like rain on a field. Now, still moving your hand, tilt it, slacken your wrist slightly, and begin to gently shake your whole arm. Seed should start to fall. As you complete one circle, move in toward the center of the flat a bit, sowing in a gradually closing spiral. Sow the edges of the flat more heavily than the center. If you want to practice first, lay a towel out on a table or the floor and sow it with grains of rice or sesame seed until you feel you're ready for the real thing. Try to let the seed fall evenly.

If you have a small garden, you may not need to sow more than one flat, and you can sow a number of different crops in it. In this case, however, sow in rows rather than in a spiral. Plants like lettuce that germinate and grow rapidly and will be ready for transplanting into the bed first should go close to one side so that you don't disrupt everything else when you remove them. In most cases this first group will include all the hardy spring plants like chard, broccoli, and so forth. The next row or two should be tenderer plants, like tomatoes, melons, dahlias, and bell peppers, which may in fact need to be moved into larger containers or another flat, spaced more widely apart, before they go into the garden, since it is likely they will outgrow this first flat before the weather is warm enough for them to be put outside. Finally, put slow-growing things like herbs and perennial flowers at the far side, so they can be left alone the longest.

189

When a flat has been fully sown, cover the seed with more mix. Repeat the same circular sowing motion described above, this time holding soil mix instead of seed. Cover to a depth about twice the thickness of an individual seed. In other words, just barely cover it. Don't bury it. The finer your seed is, the thinner the cover over it should be. Some seeds, like chamomile, should not be covered at all since they require light to germinate.

Water the flat often and lightly, as often as three times a day. Note, however, that the greatest hazard young seedlings face in their first home is a fungus disease called "damping-off," which occurs in conditions of too much moisture. It attacks seedlings at their collar, the point where the stem emerges from the ground, rotting it and causing the plants to keel over.

Damping-off can be fought in two ways: by increasing the proportion of sand in your soil mix, which improves drainage in the flats, and by making sure that you let the surface of a sown flat become dry between waterings. Alternations of moist and dry soil help prevent damping-off.

Within a month or less, your fast-germinating seed will have sprouted and the seedlings will be getting crowded. When a fine spring day comes along, and the soil in the garden seems to be workable and not too cold or wet, hardier spring seedlings can be transplanted directly into the beds. But if the soil in the beds isn't ready when the seedlings start to crowd each other, you'll need to move them out of their tight quarters and temporarily replant them into another flat (known as the "pricking-out" flat), spaced farther apart this time.

To remove them, whether for transplanting directly into the garden or into a pricking-out flat, you have two choices: One is to remove the board along their side of the seed flat entirely and lift out a complete section of soil and seedlings by slipping a trowel or your hand fork into the bottom of the flat, horizontally. The other is to leave the flat intact, insert your hand fork into the flat vertically, and lift out a section of seedlings. Once that first section is removed, the others will be easier to get at.

As you remove each section of soil and seedlings, drop it gently onto a firm surface — the surface of the bed or a potting table. This light quake loosens the mix and helps separate one seedling from another.

Now find two adjacent plants in the loosened segment. Holding them by the tips of their leaves and not the stem, lift and shake them apart, gently and slowly. They should separate easily and you should be able to see long white roots, with leaf mold still clinging to them here and there. The roots should be at least as long as the green growth, ideally many times as long. Discard any seedlings with short or broken-off roots.

Next slip your hand fork (or trowel) vertically down into the bed (or flat), and lever the handle forward to make a hole for the seedling. With your other hand, pick up one seedling by the tip of a leaf and hold it upright in the hole. It should be set slightly deeper in its new home than it was in the first flat. Set the fork aside, and fill in the hole around the seedling with soil. Press the soil in around the plant lightly with your fingertips. It's best to transplant in the later afternoon or on an overcast day.

Whether they are being transplanted into a bed or another flat, set plants out in the triangular pattern shown below, where each plant is placed opposite the space between the plants on either side of it.

New transplants should be watered immediately after being set out. Use a small watering can or something similar

Triangular spacing of plants   Planting a seedling

(a tin can will do fine) with a pointed spout that delivers a stream of water, not a spray. If you can, use tepid rather than cold water (collected in a rain barrel, for example). Direct the water to the base of each plant, so that its leaves don't get wet. (An alternative method for watering plants in flats is to put the entire flat in a tub or basin, fill it with an inch or two of water, and let the moisture soak upwards from below.)

Summer Again

In the summer of your second year, you focus on much the same things as in the first year: observation, pest control, and harvest.

Pest control. In your first year you grew easy crops, annuals mostly, that come up quickly and are just as quickly harvested, giving bugs and diseases little time to gain a foothold. In the second and later years, however, as you begin to repeat crops and to grow more perennials, you will find that you have to be more alert for such pests and problems as leaf miners in the strawberries, rust in the asparagus, fireblight on the apples, and brown rot in the plums.

Your basic controls remain the same. Close observation is still the key to success. Knowing each crop and its possible problems, and *identifying them early* if they occur will save lots of trouble. The first thing is simply to check the garden regularly. You will know when something is amiss — when holes first start to show up in a leaf, or when its edges begin to curl.

Fruit crops, in particular, are more susceptible to pests than most other home garden crops, and keeping the area around them free of fallen fruit and leaves is of the utmost importance. After their first year in your garden, it's a good idea to collect any diseased leaves from them and burn them or dispose of them in a garbage can or dumpster. Also, leaves that fall to the ground should be collected and put in the center of a compost pile that is still working.

As plants evolve their intricate, active relationships with the environment, including pests and diseases, many develop sophisticated self-defense systems, including substances that function as natural pesticides. Research into the use of these substances in the garden, a field called "companion planting," is of particular interest to gardeners who want to sidestep the complications of synthetic chemicals. That some plants exert potent influences on other plants is well known. Walnut trees, for example, exude a substance called juglone that suppresses the growth of many species unlucky enough to throw seed under their canopies. Marigolds, according to one specialist, "have reduced populations of *Meloidogyne pratylenus* and other nematode genera. The soil surrounding marigold plants becomes toxic and adjacent plants are at least partially protected. Asparagus,

Asparagus officinalis, contains a glycoside in the roots, stems, and leaves that is highly toxic to the nematode, *Trichodomus christei,* and several others."[1]

Some other remedies and the pests they combat include garlic plants for Japanese beetles; green beans for the Colorado potato beetle; wood ash for cucumber beetles, potato bugs, and squash borers; potatoes (and marigolds) for the Mexican bean beetle. Also, nettle increases the oil content in peppermint; fava beans turned into the beds will reduce soil fungus problems; and a simple blast of water from the hose, which disrupts their breeding cycle, dislodges aphids. The reading guide contains a number of books on this subject.

The clamp. Late summer is again the time to start thinking about harvest and storage. Many vegetables freeze well, and herbs can be kept if they are first dried. For root crops like carrots, parsnips, turnips, or beets, a traditional method called a "clamp" is fun to use.

Like most traditional garden techniques, a clamp is both easy to build and quite effective. Begin by laying down a level, circular pad of moist sand, an inch or two in depth and about a yard in diameter. Cut the green tops off the storage crop to within 1 to 2 inches of the top of the root. Then put down a 360-degree fan of the crop, tips pointing inward toward the center. Lay another inch of slightly moist sand on top of the first layer of roots, then another layer of the crop, and so on, to a maximum height of 2 to 3 feet. The diameter of each succeeding layer should decrease somewhat, making the shape of the final result more like a cone than a cylinder.

Root crops stored in a clamp and kept cool and just slightly moist will stay fresh for as long as two months.

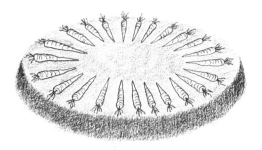

Clamp

Later in the year, you can hold or "clamp" root crops directly in the ground by putting a very thick mulch over them. Wait until the carrots are ready to harvest and winter approaches. Then cover them with an insulating blanket of leaves or straw. A month or two later, as other nearby ground freezes, you will be able to push away the mulch and pull carrots from soil that is still loose.

Container Gardening

Of course, not everyone has the land for a garden. Even if you don't have a patch of ground, however, you can usually find room for a pot or two on the roof, the deck, or a windowsill.

The first thing to consider is the container. Unglazed clay pots are best, in my view, for the same reason that I like double-dug soil: because they breathe. They allow moisture and air to pass in and out of the soil mix they contain. By contrast, other kinds of pots, such as those made of plastic or glazed earthenware, do not. They may dry out less rapidly, but they also tend to encourage waterlogged roots and fungus diseases. Extra attention to watering is well worth the advantages of clay, as far as I'm concerned. Planter boxes made of redwood, cedar, or cypress are also good, for

195

the same reason. These woods have the advantage of being rot-resistant.

Once you've chosen your container, the next step is to think about the mix. If you have the components available, I strongly recommend that you use the seed flat mix I describe earlier in this chapter — one-third loamy garden soil, one-third sharp sand, and one-third leaf mold — and that you also use compost and naturally occurring amendments for fertilizing your container plants. This will help develop the soil life in the container.

However, people who have no land to garden in are unlikely to have access to loam, sand, leaves, and compost. As an alternative, make use of what you can find at your local nursery or greenhouse. In most cases this will be a prepackaged potting mix, made up mainly of peat moss, vermiculite, and, sometimes, soil.

These mixes do have advantages: They are lightweight and can take frequent watering without compacting. If they do contain soil, it will be sterilized. It also means, however, that what you put in your pot will not be a living thing, like soil. Instead it will be a neutral medium that holds the roots, gives the plant support, and conveys the water and nutrients you add. It will not, in and of itself, be nutritious. You will have to supply whatever nutrition your plants are going to get, and you will most likely need to use synthetic fertilizers (and pesticides). Do so in a restrained way, using a time-released fertilizer, preferably one with a low, "complete" formulation, like 5-10-5.

With container plants, watering is the number-one problem. In the ground, roots can search deeply for water if the soil is loose. Not so in a pot. The only water available is what you put there. The roots also need air as much as they need water, and can drown or rot if they're constantly soaking. So you have to be attentive and regular about watering, letting the soil dry some between waterings.

Drainage is thus very important. All clay pots should have a hole in the bottom for this reason. If you get one without holes, drill or punch some in it. Then place a shard or two of broken pottery, an irregularly shaped rock, or a piece of wire mesh over the hole. (This is called "crocking" and keeps the potting mix from washing out of the pot when you water. Be sure the crocking does not completely plug the hole.)

Underwatering is also a problem. Dry indoor air pulls moisture out of the pot faster than you expect, and soon the plant is suffering from drought. Both overwatering and underwatering show up as browning at the tips of the leaves. Just poke a finger in the mix to find out which it is.

Another common problem with housebound plants is dead air. Plants like fresh, gently moving air. Nurserymen used to say that the air should be "buoyant" and were very exacting about opening and closing greenhouse ventilators to get maximum air movement with minimum temperature loss. When a warm afternoon gives you the chance, set your housebound plants outside, or open a window for them.

Now you have a pot that breathes, and a mix that is fibrous and bouncy, one that will take a lot of watering without getting compressed. The next thing you need to do is consider your site. Spend some time out on the patio feeling the sun's heat, taking note of how the rain washes off the roof, checking the difference in temperature next to a reflective white stucco wall compared to a heat-retentive dark red brick one.

When you know the site, you will make better selections of plants suited to it. A north- or east-facing wall, for example, favors plants requiring less sun and cooler temperatures than a south- or west-facing wall. Describe your location to a nursery and ask for advice.

Almost anything will grow in pots, even trees if the container is large enough. It's best, in my view, to select plants that grow naturally in your area, ones that would grow outside if you put them there, or those that will like the still air of a house. Just because something shows up in a local greenhouse does not necessarily mean that it is appropriate for your home or patio. Most greenhouses are run as controlled tropical environments, with high humidity levels, frequent watering, regular fumigation, and so forth. They provide a very different environment from the dry interior of a home or the windy, exposed condition of a patio or deck.

In cool, humid regions, ferns, azaleas, cyclamens, and other woodland plants — even mosses — will not be difficult to grow in containers. In drier, brighter zones, spring bulbs or plants from Asia Minor, Mexico, or the Southwest, like cacti and some of the penstemons, will make good selections. I think sweet-scented plants are also ideal for pot culture, because their fragrance pervades the house in the evening. Lilies, mignonette, and nicotiana are good choices.

But herbs are my favorite container plants. First, because they're tough. They can withstand dry conditions and occasional neglect. Second, their foliage and fragrance are a strong reminder of nature. And finally, they are not only attractive but useful as well, for cooking, home remedies (I wouldn't be without aloe vera), tea, lavender sachets for the linen closet, and much more.

Oregano, rosemary, and parsley are all good choices, but basil is my favorite. I start new basil seed every spring in pots and transplant the seedlings into the garden. Then, when cold weather approaches in the fall, I dig up a well-grown plant or two, cut them back hard, and pot them in 6- to 8-inch pots, which then go on the sill of a south-facing window for the winter. When I dig up a plant to bring it inside for the winter, I add a little compost or fertilizer around the roots, and water it right away. Through the winter, I sometimes empty my tea leaves or coffee grounds into the pot for the nutrients and mulch. Whenever I want fresh pesto, the main ingredient is right there.

A pesto recipe I like:

Collect two cups of fresh basil.

Cut the leaves from the stems, and put them in a blender.

Add ½ cup extra-virgin olive oil, 2 tablespoons of chopped English walnuts (or pine nuts), a teaspoon of salt, and 2 cloves of pressed garlic.

Run the blender at medium speed until the basil is pureed.

Pour into a mixing bowl. (Scrape every particle out of the blender.)

Coarsely grate ½ cup of Parmesan cheese, then add 2 tablespoons of some other cheese (like Romano or Gruyère).

Stir the cheese into the basil with a spoon.

Also stir in 3 tablespoons of softened butter.

Refrigerate.

Bring to room temperature before serving.

Great with all kinds of pasta, on slices of fresh tomato, or in pesto, tomato, and bacon sandwiches.

How can you tell if a container plant is healthy or not? In general, it should be a deep, lustrous green, which shows that it is getting a good supply of nutrients and photosynthesizing well. Closely spaced branches and leaves and even coloring are also good signs.

TWELVE

Real Wealth

*W*hen I left the Garden Project at Santa Cruz, I knew what I wanted to do: I wanted to be a market gardener, and so without further ado I went to southern Missouri, to make a garden on a forty-acre piece of land in the foothills of the Ozarks.

The first thing I learned was that there was a lot I didn't know. I knew that Alan's methods had originated, in part, in the Paris market gardens of eighty years ago, but I did not realize that in America market gardening (or "truck farming," as it used to be called) had pretty much gone the way of the dodo, eclipsed by the age of the big farm. To my mind, the Garden Project had been so astonishingly productive I thought it would work anywhere, if one wanted to do that sort of thing. And I wanted to do that sort of thing.

I also didn't know how much work it would be for me, working alone, to start a garden. There had been droves of people working in the Santa Cruz garden. There was but one in mine. And the soil in that part of the Ozark foothills turned out to be more rock than dirt. But I persevered. After a couple of years of godawful digging, I had formed terraces on a southeast slope and built walls and steps of jagged stone. I remember looking at the old stone farmhouses in that part of the country with new respect.

The garden was prolific from the beginning. Although my plot of ground was forty acres in size, I only worked one-half acre intensively. On the rest I followed a rigorous no-till policy — I left it alone. There I took walks, watching the young oaks and underground streams springing out of the earth after a hard rain, in the quiet of the woods. The rest of the time, like Thoreau, I hoed my beans and thought about important things.

I hadn't paid much attention in my plunge into gardening to the reality of the word *market*. At first I found I couldn't sell what I grew. One time I took a basket of Swiss chard to the jail in Pineville. The next time I stopped by, I was told not to bring any more — the inmates had refused to eat it. Eventually I did find a reliable buyer, a local religious community called Shiloh Farms, whose members were themselves involved in making and selling whole-grain breads and other health foods. They were happy to buy all I could grow — my snow peas, Bibb lettuce, Japanese radishes, string beans, and cantaloupes — for their own kitchens.

Loneliness, however, turned out to be the worst thing I had overlooked about the life of a market gardener in a part of the country where my nearest neighbors were few and almost invariably fifty years my elder. I was, for the first time in my life, alone. Most days, only one person passed by on my road, a neighbor who went to work early in the morning and returned at 4:30. Otherwise, no human noise save my own competed with the birds, the crickets, and the stream.

I worked in that garden for three years, time I in no way regret, solitary as it was. From early spring to late fall, I was in the garden from early morning until night fell, nearly every day. The labor was hard, but there were real rewards in it. As Thoreau did, I learned that cutting my own firewood warmed me twice, and that the first time was indeed the "most wholesome and memorable." The second reward came at night, when I put the logs into my potbellied stove, imprinted with the seal of the Great Western Company. When the flames lit up its mica windows, I knew I was done for the day.

Eventually the need for companionship grew too strong and I left to rejoin the world. The idea of market gardening has stayed with me, however, and I'm inclined to think that, despite overwhelming evidence to the contrary, the day of the very small farmer may again be at hand. As I like to imagine it, a tour of my next market garden would go something like this:

"Welcome. You've picked a fine day for a visit. Let's take this path and I'll show you what we've been doing here at Hedgerow Farms for the last five years.

"First, if you'll bear with me, a bit of background as we walk. I had long wanted to have a large market garden and nursery business. Ever since the early 1970s, in fact, about twenty-five years ago now. The main obstacles were, as you might guess, economic. Land was hard to come by, and expensive when it was available. And then there were the start-up costs and the expenses to carry while we were building up the soil, improving our ability to grow high-quality market produce, and establishing our long-term crops: asparagus, fruit trees, and berries. And there was also the need, which I learned about long ago, to cultivate our market as well, to find steady customers who would reliably buy what we grew.

"Well, as you can see, we've done it. There's a total of

twenty-five acres here, and we're not that far from our main market, Lawrence. We found that hillside country tended to be a bit cheaper than the flatlands here in Kansas, mainly because the latter are easier to farm with heavy machinery. Just beyond those wooded hills over there is the Kaw River.

"My main economic strategy can be summed up in one word: Diversity. First of all, Hedgerow Farms operates as a school. We take in half a dozen or so apprentices each fall, some of whom arrived yesterday. Having students doesn't bring in all that much, once you subtract expenses from their tuition, but it most definitely does keep our labor costs low, and that gives us the capacity to price our stuff competitively. Also, and even more important, it gives us a feeling of community here, a sense of shared purpose, and that means a great deal to me. The first time I tried market gardening I did it all by myself.

"Our main source of cash income is our mail-order nursery, which we'll take a closer look at later. We concentrate on rock-garden plants, herbs, and certain perennials. Some of our varieties are special, such as a strain of cherry tomato and a pastel hollyhock that were both developed at the Chadwick gardens in Santa Cruz. You've never heard of Chadwick? Well, I've got a book you can read that'll give you a feel for his approach. Remind me to give you a copy later.

"OK, here we are. From the top of this rise you can see most of Hedgerow Farms. Those hills straight across this little valley mark the beginning of the woodland that almost completely encircles us and accounts for about half of our total acreage here. We get timber and firewood there, and we use it as a classroom. That's where the apprentices and I go to see nature uncultivated, to remind us of the original lessons that underlie everything we do here. It's also a pre-

serve of sorts, for birds and other kinds of wildlife. I'm of
the view that if we get too manipulative down in the gardens, we'll be able to find something there that will put us
back on the right track.

"I say 'down in the gardens,' and as you can see, that's literally the case. Down in the valley is our main area of cultivated beds and fields, some eighteen acres all told. Where
the hills level off into the valleys around here is where you
can find the deepest topsoil and the sites that are least liable
to erode. Our first year here we just plowed all that acreage
down there, sowed it to vetch and rye, then plowed all the
new growth right back under the next spring, for green
compost. Worked like a charm.

"Looks kind of like an extra large backyard garden from
up here, doesn't it? This is my favorite view. That's why I
put the bench here.

"What you see down there is a real mixture: two acres of strawberries and bramble fruits, one acre of beds for our mail-order crops, five acres of field crops. This year we grew tomatoes, sweet corn, soybeans, and winter squash, five acres of pasture and herbal ley, an acre and a half of intensive beds for mixed vegetables, herbs, and both cut and perennial flowers, plus, as you can see, a greenhouse, a potting shed, a water tank, cold frames, compost piles, and a work area for our nursery. Like I said, *diversity.*

"Twice a month we take produce and flowers into the farmer's market in Lawrence. As a matter of fact, we're getting ready for one tomorrow. They've become a big thing these last few years, farmer's markets, and that's one of our more important sources of income. Flowers are actually more profitable for us than vegetables. Cosmos, for instance, bring in $4.00 a bunch, and it's usually pretty easy for us to sell forty bunches in a single morning at the market, forty bunches that take at most two hours for one of the apprentices to gather. You can see a couple of them down there right now, doing just that.

"Herbs also sell fairly well at the market, but our best customers for those crops are local restaurants. That's a more predictable market, and we save time because we don't have to wash and tie lots of small bundles. Basil, chives, and French tarragon are the most popular. Ever tried French tarragon? I'll give you some to take with you this afternoon. It tastes like anise.

"Let's see, what else have we got down there? Oh yes, the berries. Now that's another crop that's turned out to be a good income source for us, and one that's easy to manage to boot. Those we sell — along with the fruit in some small patches of melons — on a pick-your-own basis. When we first started doing that, we just opened up those parts of the farm to anyone who wanted to drive up here. But the program turned out to be so popular that we soon had more people showing up than we could handle, so we started selling subscriptions. That's worked out very well. We charge a yearly fee of $50.00, and at last count I believe we had a little over 100 families enrolled. In June they come for the strawberries, in July for raspberries and blackberries, and in August for the melons. We assign them weekends so they don't all come at the same time. Most bring their kids and a lunch and make a day of it. That trail at the lower end of the valley leads to a picnic area by a little lake. A lot of those people also buy milk and other produce from us, and I sell a few customers — the serious gardeners — some of my precious compost.

"Let's see, is that all? Pardon me? Oh, those white boxes are beehives. We have eighteen now. Also, although you can't see it from here, we do have an orchard, just around that bend at the upper end of the valley. Most of our trees are just now coming into bearing, so we don't know yet how well that part of our business will do, but we're optimistic. We plan to ship the fruit to specialty markets and gourmet shops, at high prices. All our varieties were chosen for their superior flavor and will be ripened on the tree. Nothing in the supermarket will be able to rival them for taste. We have old-fashioned varieties, like the Belle of Georgia peach and Count Althann's gage plum, as well as the more recently developed, disease-resistant types, like the Nova Easygro apple. Two of last year's apprentices got so interested in growing fruit trees they bought five acres adjoining us up there and are going into the fruit tree nursery business. They'll also be taking on some of the teaching duties here. Let's walk on down now and take a closer look at the nursery and a few other things down in the gardens. . . .

"Well, here we are. Nice little hike, isn't it? Let's start with the greenhouse. No, after you, thanks. . . . Oh, I see some of the new apprentices are here. Would you excuse me for just a moment while I give them instructions? . . .

"Good morning, everyone, and let me say again how much I'm looking forward to our coming year together. I hope your stay at Hedgerow Farms will be rewarding. As you know, Lee and Brigitte here are returning from last year, so please feel free to ask them for help. I trust you've found your accommodations in the Old Barn, and that you're comfortable. If you need anything in that respect, please see Dessie.

"What we need to do today is prepare for our semi-monthly trip to the farmer's market in Lawrence. First, we have to cut as many flowers as possible. I know Lee and Henry have already been hard at work at that task since breakfast, and I'd like to see it finished within the hour. In the meantime, Waldo and Steve, would you please continue with the herb gathering, and would Brigitte and Beth keep gathering seed? After lunch, Lee, Henry, Waldo, Steve, and I will turn our attention to the squash field. There are about 1,700 squash out there, or a little over 4 tons. At 40 cents a pound, that crop is worth $3,000 to us, so let's do our level best to get it in the truck before nightfall. OK, that's it, thank you. . . .

"As you can see, our apprentices are put to work right away. Fall is one of our busiest seasons — as well as harvesting crops, they'll also be busy preparing the beds for fall sowing. For example, next week we'll start preparing seed beds outdoors for sowing alpines before winter. Nowadays, researchers are trying to develop special technologies to hurry germination, but I prefer making seed beds and sowing the seed outside where winter will freeze and thaw the ground and tell the seed that this is the right place, the right time to come out. It may take longer that way, and be more labor-intensive, but it's also more satisfying, like double-digging. When winter actually settles in, so will we, doing greenhouse work and studying basic horticulture and small-farm management. Then come next spring, it'll be plant-ings, shipping out our mail-order sales, and taking care of newborn chicks.

"If you'll just step over here and glance out that window, you'll see Lee and Henry bringing the flowers they've cut to the cleaning shed, over there under the water tank. Shaded by the cool water, it never gets higher than 55 degrees inside that shed in the fall, and flowers set out in cans of cold water will keep quite well for a day or two. We also clean seed in there. I'll show you that in a bit. First, let's walk on through the greenhouse, toward the other end.

"Yes, there are quite a few different things in here. Di-versity, that's our watchword. Hmm? Oh, those are prim-roses. Come back when they bloom, next spring. They're descendents of the pale yellow Munstead strain, first devel-oped by Gertrude Jekyll.

"Just through here is the potting shed. Watch your step. I have a special thing about potting sheds. If I had to name any single spot as the heart of Hedgerow Farms, this would be it. This is where the day begins and ends for me. As you can see, we store a lot of the ingredients for our potting mixes here, because they have to be kept out of the ele-ments and protected from freezing. In these bins we've got leaf mold, sharp sand, turf loam, and vermiculite, as well as sphagnum moss for packing around the roots of our mail-order shipments. All the composts are watered or misted from time to time to keep them just slightly damp. Moisture is important to their soil life.

"We also store our tools in here, as you can see. The potting shed is always kept in orderly condition, with the tools in their places, in good repair, well oiled, clean, and sharp. That way, when we go to dig potatoes, we know that the forks are right there. When we go to pick berries, we know that the baskets are right here. It's efficient — not the efficiency of the factory, but the efficiency of purposeful human activity.

"That big table over there is our potting bench. That's where we do most of our transplanting and where we prepare mail-order shipments. Notice how the top of the bench comes to a height that's about 5 or 6 inches below my elbows. That's so I can work at it for hours without straining my back.

"Any questions, just ask. That? Oh, that's our garden log. It's very important to record quite a lot of different kinds of information — sowing dates, rainy weather, etc. — in an operation like ours, and to do so on the spot, as soon as we think of it. Otherwise, we forget things. It's just too much to keep in mind at the end of the day, when we're tired.

"I love it in here, with the woodsy smell of all those mixes, and the endless potential of all those bags of seed in the next room. It's a great place for puttering. As the weather gets worse, we'll find ourselves spending more and more time in here, sharpening the secateurs, transplanting, planning for next year.

"Yes, it does smell good in here, doesn't it? That's from the seeds. I'll show you how we collect seed in a moment or two, and you'll understand how it is that there are some flower parts and husks still mixed in with the seed. I'm very fond of that fragrance myself. In fact, that's probably one of the main reasons I come here so often, checking on things — that and the fact that it's so quiet in here.

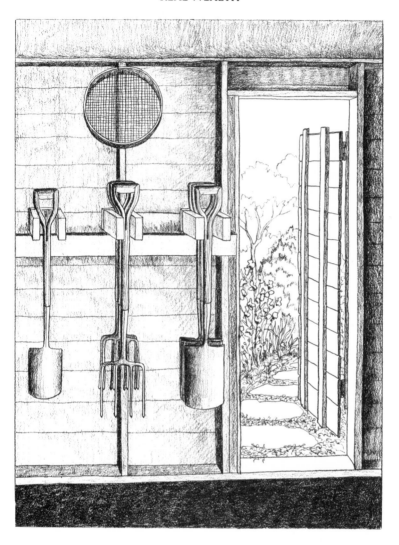

"Oh, there're thousands of seeds in all those little bags. More than I want to count. That's our real wealth. The garden seeds — the flowers and vegetables — are kept on the north wall. Over there are the seeds for our nursery business. I've even saved some of the seed from the wildflowers and other plants that were here before we first started plowing. And then people send us seed, and I trade seed for unusual and old-fashioned varieties. A lot of it has been in here since the shed was built; we don't have the time or space to grow it all. Shall we walk on out to the squash field now? . . .

"This is one of our most important harvests. We grow the Waltham butternut squash, for several reasons. First, it sells well. Second, it stores well: what we don't sell we'll be able to keep through the winter. Third, this particular squash was bred to be resistant to the squash vine borer; specifically, the vine was developed to be so tough and woody the borer can't get into it. Finally, we grow it because the taste is excellent. We bake it, make it into a pie that tastes better than pumpkin pie, and serve it as a hearty soup.

"OK, here we are. As you can see, we planted the squash in 30-foot-wide strips. That 6-foot path between each strip is planted in white clover. The paths are for the wagon we use to collect the squash. The clover is low growing, so it doesn't impede the wagon. Also, its roots help fix nitrogen in the soil, which has been of great help to the squash all summer in developing all that lush foliage, and finally, as we harvest the squash, the horses are happy to browse the clover while we work.

"We walk through the field three abreast, gathering up the squash and passing them along to the person manning the wagon. Once the wagon is full, the horses will haul it up to where the truck is parked; we don't allow heavy machinery down here in the valley because it would compact the soil.

"Once the squash is harvested, we gather the vines, take them to the compost piles, and disc the whole field, turning the clover under as a green compost, again using the horses to draw the harrow. Then we sow winter rye as a cover crop.

"See those two areas tied off with red ribbon? Those squash will be saved for seed collection. In a few days we'll come back and collect them too.

"I choose the seed stock like this: As soon as the squash plants sprouted last summer, I began watching them, looking for the traits I wanted to encourage. The first one is early germination and rapid growth. That's desirable so that next year's crops will outdistance bugs and disease, and grow those tough vines as quickly as possible. I mark the most rapid growers with dated plastic labels.

"Then, as the plants continue to grow, I look for more subtle signs of special vigor: a deeper green and closer spacing of the leaves on the stem, for example. Before long, flowers appear. I look for the plants with the earliest flowering and quickest fruit-setting, and again mark those.

"Finally, I give my candidates the all-important taste test. I take some squash from each marked plant, bake half, and eat it without butter. It's the unaided flavor I'm looking for. The other half I steam and purée in a blender, then add a little milk, butter, salt, and pepper for a squash soup. Wilfred would have loved it. Who's Wilfred? Oh, an old gardening friend.

"Ultimately, selecting seed is really a matter of intuition. I save seed from a plant because I think I can sense a promise of vitality and beauty in it. Simple as it is, all our apprentices want to be in on the actual collecting of the seed, probably because I make such a big thing about it. Let's walk up to the cleaning shed. . . .

"Here, as you can see, we have large double sinks, though old washtubs would do just as well. To clean the seed, we first half-fill both sinks with tepid water. Then we cut the squash open and scrape the seed out into the first sink. The seeds are rubbed clean by hand under water, given a rinse in the second sink, and placed on an old window screen to dry. In about two weeks, they'll be dry enough to put in brown paper bags — they have to be thoroughly dry or they'll rot. We store them in the seed room, which is dry and cool, but well-enough insulated so that they won't freeze. And of course we keep the door securely closed against rats and mice, which would love nothing better than to feast on all these stored riches.

"Many plants, of course, produce a dry seed, and those we clean a little differently, using one of two methods. The first is winnowing, which simply means blowing the lighter chaff away from the seed. We do this with lettuce seed, for example, by setting an old washtub on the floor in front of an electric fan. The fan is turned on to a low or medium speed, and the collected material, held in cupped hands, is tossed a few inches up in the air, over the tub. The chaff blows away; the seed falls into the tub. The second way is by putting collected material through a sieve, rubbing it lightly so as not to injure the seed.

"Then there are also those very large seeds, like beans, peas, and hollyhocks, that can be harvested and bagged without cleaning. We just let them dry on the plant, collect them when they're ready, remove the outside pod or capsule, pop them in a bag, and we're ready for next year. Real wealth.

214

"Now, sowing seed is only one way to propagate your crops. The other is division, which basically means pulling the plant apart at the 'crown,' where the roots meet the stem, creating a number of new stem-plus-root segments. Plants that lend themselves to this kind of propagation are characterized by multiple stems, so division is only an accentuation of the way they grow and increase naturally. Each of the smaller pieces of the mother plant is then replanted in a pot, box, or nursery bed, one with very good drainage. It's quite a simple process, really.

"Lots of our herbaceous perennials — daylilies, pyrethrum, veronica, iris, scabiosa — are just about ready for division. Also, a number of the smaller alpines can be divided in early fall, including campanulas, saxifrage, and sempervivum, among others. We'll also be dividing some herbs: chives, hyssop, lavender, lemon balm, sorrel, and thyme. Potted up now, they'll be ready for sale next spring.

"Here, want to divide this lemon balm? We lifted it this

Lemon-balm division

215

morning from a bed outside and stuck it in this pile of soil mix to keep it from drying out. OK, first drop it on the floor here a couple of times to loosen it up. Now, stick these two forks into the middle of it, back to back, and pry the clump apart. The smaller clumps you can pull apart by hand. Now repeat the dividing until we've got a dozen pieces or so. Good, that's it. Simple, isn't it?

"Later on, we'll put those segments into 4-inch plastic pots and water them. Then we'll set those plants, still in the pots, into an uncovered cold frame and bury them up to their rims with composted sawdust. They will root this fall, and fill out nicely by spring, just in time to be sold. . . .

"Well, that's the tour. Thanks for stopping by. You have your copy of the book, I see, and some of that French tarragon. Oh, and here's some information about our apprentice program at Hedgerow Farms. Drop by again, anytime."

Catalogues, Seeds, Plants, Tools, and More

Seeds and Plants

Burpee
Warminister, PA 18974
One of America's leading seedhouses.

Park Seed
Box 31
Greenwood, SC 29646
Another big company. I like the culture guide in the middle of this catalogue.

Necessary Trading Company
New Castle, VA 24127
General garden supplies, including biological controls, natural fertilizers, tools, and books as well as seeds.

Bountiful Gardens
5798 Ridgewood Rd.
Willits, CA 95490
John Jeavons's catalogue carries Chase Organic seeds. ($1.00)

Nichols Garden Nursery
1190 N. Pacific Hwy
Albany, OR 97321
Herbs, old-fashioned and gourmet vegetables. ($1.00)

William Dam
Box 8400
Dundas, Ontario L9H 6M1
Canada
Untreated seed, fine variety selection.

Rocky Mountain Seed Co.
1325 15th St.
Denver, CO 80217
They sell mail-order, mostly in the region. I list this item to emphasize again the value of regional seedhouses.

Herb Gathering
5742 Kenwood
Kansas City, MO 64110
Gourmet, French vegetable varieties.

Johnny's Selected Seed
Albion, ME 04910
Especially good for the Northeast. ($1.00)

Seeds Blum
Idaho City Storage
Boise, ID 83707
Heirloom seeds, fine old-fashioned varieties. ($1.00)

Redwood City Seeds
Box 361
Redwood City, CA 94064
Especially suited to California. ($1.00)

Earl May Seed and Nursery
Shenandoah, IA 51603

Thompson and Morgan
Box 100
Farmingdale, NJ 07727
Old, large firm, tremendous list, especially of flowers.

Di Giorgi Co.
Box 413
Council Bluffs, IA 51502
(*$1.00*)

Herbst Seedsmen
1000 N. Main
Brewster, NY 10509

Fruit and Fruit Trees

Henry Leuthardt
Montauk Hwy
East Morishes, Long Island, NY 11940
Dwarf and espalier garden trees. ($1.00)

Southmeadow Fruit Gardens
Lakeside, MI 49116
Their variety and price list is free. However, you will also want the descriptive Illustrated Catalog, *$8.00.*

New York State Fruit Testing Cooperative Association
Box 462
Geneva, NY 14456
$5.00 for membership and catalogue.

W. F. Allen
Salisbury, MD 21801
Strawberries, raspberries, asparagus, etc. ($1.00)

Applesource
Tom Vorbeck
Rt. One
Chapin, IL 62628
This is not a fruit tree nursery; it's a mail-order source for the apples themselves. They come boxed from specialist growers. Great gifts, and a good way to taste an old-time apple if you're thinking of planting one.

Stark Bros.
Louisiana, MO 63353

APPENDIX A

Specialist Growers

Roses

Roses of Yesterday and Today
802 Brown's Valley Rd.
Watsonville, CA 95076
An attractive, well-written catalogue of old and rare roses. Get your order in early. ($2.00)

High Country Rosarium
717 Downing St.
Denver, CO 80218
This is a mail-order specialist in my neighborhood. Check around in your area for small nurseries. ($1.00)

Pickering Nurseries
670 Kingston Rd.
Pickering, Ontario L1V 1A6
Canada

Lowe's Own Root Roses
6 Sheffield Rd.
Nashua, NH 03062
($1.00)

Herbs

Meadowbrook Herb Garden
Wyoming, RI 02898
Biodynamic seeds and products. ($1.00)

Taylor's Herb Gardens
1535 Lone Oak Rd.
Vista, CA 92083

Sandy Mush Herb Nursery
Rt. 2
Surrett Cove Rd.
Leicester, NC 28748

Fox Hill Farms
444 W. Michigan Ave.
Box 7
Parma, MI 49269-0007

Rock Garden and Wildflowers

Siskiyou Rare Plant Nursery
2825 Cumming Rd.
Medford, OR 97501
Extensive, elegant listing of hardy alpine and woodland plants. ($1.50)

Plants of the Southwest
1812 Second St.
Sante Fe, NM 87501
In addition to dryland wildflowers (suitable for the garden as well as naturalizing), they have a marvelous selection of ancient and modern vegetables for the Southwest. ($1.00)

Far North Gardens
15621 Auburndale Ave.
Livonia, MI 48154
Rare flower seed. They carry Barnhaven Primroses. ($1.25)

Barnhaven
Brigsteer, Kendal
Cumbria, LA8 8AU
England
Primrose seed. Best-written catalogue, gives insight into high-level nursery ways. ($2.00)

Perennial Flowers

Wayside Gardens
Hodges, SC 29695
Encyclopedic color catalogue. ($1.00)

White Flower Farm
Litchfield, CT 06759
($5.00)

Bluestone Perennials
7211 Ridge Rd.
Madison, OH 44057

Country Garden
Rt. 2, Box 455A
Crivitz, WI 54114

Bulbs

John Scheepers
63 Wall St.
New York, NY 10005
All kinds, especially dahlias.

McClure & Zimmerman
1422 W. Thorndale
Chicago, IL 60660
Tulips, daffodils, and more.

Messeleer
County Rd., Rt. 1-A
Box 269
Ipswich, MA 01938

Rex Bulb Farm
Box 774
Port Townsend, WA 98368
Lilies. ($1.00)

Vermont Bean Seed Co.
Holland Road
Bomoseen, VT 05732

Swan Island Dahlias
P.O. Box 800
Canby, OR 97013
($2.00)

Others

Kurt Bluemel
2543 Hess Rd.
Fallston, MD 21047
Ornamental grasses.

Gilbert Wild and Son
Sarcoxie, MO 64862
Peonies, iris, and daylilies. ($2.00)

Louis Smirnow and Son
85 Linden Lane, Glen Head P.O.
Bookville, Long Island, NY 11545
Herbaceous and tree peonies. ($1.00)

Greer Gardens
1280 Good Pasture Island Rd.
Eugene, OR 97401
Rhododendrons, azaleas, Japanese maples, and companions.

E. B. Nauman
324 Avalon Dr.
Rochester, NY 14618
Rhododendrons, azaleas, and broadleaf evergreens. ($.50)

Gossler Farms Nursery
1200 Weaver Rd.
Springfield, OR 97477
Magnolias, maples, and associated plants. ($1.00)

Natural Lawn Care

Ringer Research
6860 Flying Cloud Dr.
Eden Prairie, MN 55344
Tools, compost starter, and organic fertilizers for lawn and garden.

APPENDIX A

Tools

Smith & Hawken
25 Corte Madera
Mill Valley, CA 94941
Bulldog tools and much more.

Brookstone
300 Vose Farm Rd.
Peterborough, NH 03458

Clapper
1125 Washington St.
West Newton, MA 02165

Green River Tools
5 Cotton Mill Hill
P.O. Box 1919
Brattleboro, VT 05301

A catalogue of catalogues, listing businesses oriented to natural methods and old-time varieties, is available from:
The Graham Center Seed and Nursery Directory
Rural Advancement Fund
P.O. Box 1029
Pittsboro, NC 27312 *($2.00)*

Places That Teach the Chadwick Method

Agroecology Program
College Eight, University of California
Santa Cruz, CA 95064
Certificate program through University of California Extension, and degree-granting curricula through Environmental Studies and other departments.

John Jeavons
Ecology Action
5798 Ridgewood Rd.
Willits, CA 95490

A research center and working market garden, Ecology Action also trains apprentices who are committed to sustainable, small-scale food production and who plan to teach the method to others. A minimum commitment of one year is required and three years is recommended. ($2.00 for the preliminary application)

Timberline Farm
Rt. 2
Box 67-2
Camden, WV 26338

Teaches the biointensive approach in cooperation with Ecology Action. Format similar to the Willits minifarm. ($2.00 for preliminary application)

Gasconade Farm
Alan York, Director
Paydown Rd.
Vienna, MO 65582

Sponsored by the American Farm Foundation, this market-garden farm trains apprentices to operate a market-garden business. Minimum commitment: two years.

Steve and Gloria Decater
Star Rt.
Covelo, CA 95428

This 25-acre farm was begun when the Chadwick garden was nearby. They have a big raised-bed garden, a wide variety of animals, and a farm with horses. One or two apprentices each year.

Camp Joy
Jim and Beth Nelson
131 Camp Joy Rd.
Boulder Creek, CA 95006

Written up in the April 1973 issue of Organic Gardening, *they're still at it, growing vegetables and flowers, raising goats, and more. Write for current apprenticeship arrangements. ($2.00 and SASE)*

Saratoga Community Garden
P.O. Box 756
Saratoga, CA 95070
Write for current training program. ($2.00 and SASE)

Naropa Institute
2130 Arapahoe
Boulder, CO 80302
Offers introductory gardening classes. The Institute combines study of contemplative discipline with academic work. Write for course listings.

Green Gulch Farm
Zen Center
Star Rt. 1
Sausalito, CA 94965
A Zen Buddhist center, Green Gulch has a big garden originally inspired by Alan Chadwick in 1972.

There are many other places across the country that teach raised-bed and French intensive methods. A good place to ask about them is at a regional botanic garden.

Soil-Testing Laboratories

Your local cooperative or county extension service.

Woods End Laboratory
Box 65
Temple, ME 04984
Soil analysis for nutrients and organic matter, including chromatograms for biodynamic-oriented growers.

Sources of Major Nutrients

All gardeners, organic or chemical, must supply their crops with the major nutrients, nitrogen, phosphorus, and potassium. These naturally occurring chemical components are symbolized by the letters N, P, and K, respectively, and if you buy a bag of fertilizer it will list them, in that order. For example, if the "guaranteed analysis" reads 20-10-10, you know that 20 percent of the ingredients are nitrogen, 10 percent phosphorus, and 10 percent potassium. (The remaining 60 percent is inert substances.) Bagged organic fertilizer will carry the same numbers. Bone meal, for instance, might be 4-10-0.

Some organic sources of *nitrogen* are:

Animal manures
Fresh-cut green grass and young green leaves
Bloodmeal
Cottonseed meal
Green matter turned into the ground (called "green manure")
Fish meal or fish emulsion
Compost
Bone meal
Legume crops

Some organic sources of *phosphorus* are:

Bone meal
Rock phosphate
Animal manure
Compost (comfrey is an especially good source)

Some organic sources of *potassium* are:

Wood ash
Granite dust
Greensand
Turned-in green matter (especially alfalfa)
Green-grass clippings
Seaweed
Cottonseed meal
Compost

Suppliers of Natural Fertilizers and Organic Pesticides

The Necessary Trading Company
New Castle, VA 21427
This company carries a full line of natural pest controls, including insect-monitoring traps, Bacillus thuringiensis, *and a rotenone-pyrethrum blend. Especially valuable is their "Bio-Selector" chart, which lists appropriate measures for 40 different pests.*

Zook and Ranck, Inc.
Box 243, Dept. E
RD 1
Gap, PA 17527

Ringer Research
6860 Flying Cloud Dr.
Eden Prairie, MN 55344

Natural Development Co.
Box 215
Bainbridge, PA 17502

Barth's
Valley Stream, NY 11580

FMC Agricultural Chemical Corp.
6065 Roswell Rd., NE
Atlanta, GA 30328
Carries KOLO and liquid sulfur/clay mix for scab.

Reuter Laboratories
P.O. Box 346
Haymarket, VA 22069-0346

I especially recommend the following two organizations, but not because of their pesticides. They don't have any. Rather, this group has developed special sprays from animal, vegetable, and mineral components composted together that encourage health and plant resistance to pests and disease.

Biodynamic Preparations
RD 1
Stroudsburg, PA 18360

The Biodynamic Association
Box 253
Wyoming, RI 02898

Frankly, I have very little problem with pests and disease in growing vegetables, flowers, and herbs. Fruit bushes and trees are probably where sprays are most required. (For a minimal spray schedule, consult the Spring 1984 issue of *Biodynamics*, No. 150, pp. 35–40.)

A Note on Pesticide Use

As you can probably tell, I'm not a great fan of pesticides, organic or otherwise. All pesticides work best as preventives. I prefer to put my preventive efforts into the health of the garden as a whole rather than risk the side effects of a poison. Good preventive measures are crop rotation; growing many different species (especially lots of herbs); selecting resistant varieties; providing good water, sunshine, and nutrition; and compost, compost, compost. Also, I grow potent plants throughout the garden rather than spray them in concentrated forms. Rather than spray nicotine sulphate, for example, I grow nicotiana. It's a lovely, fragrant flower. I also plant *Chrysanthemum cineriafolium*, from which pyrethrum is derived.

If you feel an urge to spray preventives (and I have felt that protective instinct, as all gardeners have), use the biodynamic preparations and herbal sprays first. Using a devastating insecticide often does more than just kill the bandit you're after. It may also destroy more beneficial predators and honeybees. Even killing *all* the pests may boomerang on you: without any pests for the beneficial species to dine on, they will go elsewhere, and your garden will be unprotected.

If, especially for economic reasons, you must spray, identify problems early and accurately and use a treatment specific to the pest. Neighboring gardeners and the extension service will know which pests are the big problems in your area. Still, don't be casual with a poison just because it is "organic." In fact, many of the organics are broad-spectrum and will kill a wide range of insects, whereas chemical formulations are becoming ever more pest-specific.

Design Exercise: A Sense of Place

Part 3 described how I go about gardening. Those chapters took you through the basic steps of making a backyard garden, one that has vegetables, flowers, herbs, and some plants in containers as well as trees and shrubs. The principles I'm stressing — observation, getting to know individual plants and their native homes, soil cultivation, hand labor, the cycle of growth and decay, and so on — constitute an approach to gardening that is broadly applicable. From rock gardens to greenhouses to arboretums, you will feel at home in many different kinds of gardens, if you feel at home in a well-run backyard garden.

As I showed in chapter 10, you can begin to dig beds and make compost before you have a fully worked out plan. In fact, your plans will grow and change as you garden. However, from the start, thoughts will run through your head about how to lay out your garden, so in this section I am going to show you a garden design, one for a suburban backyard. In this small space, the principles I emphasized in the "Garden Masters" section of this book can be applied. These four principles — and the gardeners who represent them — are guidelines you can use in making your own garden plan.

They are:

Design Principle	Theme	Represented by
View	Genius of the place	Olmsted
Color	Artistic good cheer	Jekyll
Order	Sacred order in nature	Wilfred
Drama of balance	The unity of practical work and artistic vision	Chadwick

Here are some design principles, feelings, and plants I associate with the four great gardeners:

OLMSTED

Design Principle	Feeling/Perception
View	Affection for nature
	Contemplation
	Receptivity
	Quietude

Plant Group	Other
Trees and shrubs	Garden bench
Grass and meadows	Curving lines
	Garden journey

JEKYLL

Design Principle	Feeling/Perception
Color	Good cheer
	Beauty
	Liveliness
	Craftsmanship

Plant Group	Other
Flowers (native plants and appropriate foreign plants; cottage flowers)	Arbors
	Luxuriance
	Vines
Old-fashioned roses	Garden walks
Old-world herbs	Woodlands

WILFRED

Design Principle	*Feeling/Perception*
Order	Respect for simple things
	Tact/finesse
	Sacred order in nature
	Tradition
	Simple human warmth

Plant Group	*Other*
Herbs	Enclosed garden
Useful plants (squash, fruit trees, medicinal herbs)	Sacred space
	Walls
	Stone
	Walks
	Contemplative work

CHADWICK

Design Principle	*Feeling/Perception*
Drama of balance	Life is change
	Imagination
	Unity of formal and informal
	Aesthetic truth
	Garden as a place to live

Plant Group	*Other*
Mixed kitchen-garden and gourmet vegetables	Seed
Weeds	Compost
Flowers	Soil — raised beds
	Reverence for all life, aphids as well as actors

Of course, in real life none of the four gardeners fits into neat little boxes. Only for purposes of simplicity do I label the four principles view, color, order, and the drama of balance.

Let me demonstrate how I might plan a garden using these principles. Here is a garden layout that shows where things are

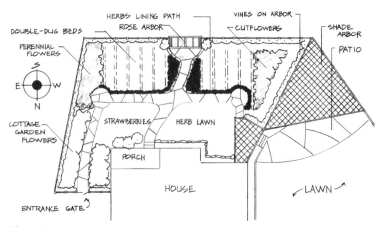

Plan view

located. This is called a plan view; it is like a map, looking at the layout from above.*

The first design principle I want to include is associated with Olmsted: the discovery and making of garden views. A view is a contemplative spot in the garden, a place where receptivity to nature is easy.

There are several important views in this garden. In fact, it is a series of views and visual pictures that lead you through the garden. Restful spots invite you to sit down and simply look at the garden. The entrance on the east leads through a collection of cottage-garden flowers. It announces that you have left the workaday world and entered a garden. It quiets the mind.

Then as the path turns the corner of the house, the view opens out to a large field and an old farmstead that borders this suburban development. The most important view is from the rose arbor. Two small benches in the arbor, for garden rest and quiet conversation, invite you to sit down. Once you are seated, the field, farmhouse, and mountains in the distance draw your attention into nature, the prime gardener, all around.

*All the drawings in this section are by Robert Howard.

Having established the garden boundaries and a sense of visual journey through it, the next step is to enliven it with color. Call on the spirit of Miss Jekyll to lend her wit and good cheer to the garden plan. I've already mentioned the cottage-garden flowers on the east walk, which include peonies, lupine, iris, and matted thymes in the flagstone walk.

At the west end of the garden are cut flowers and opposite them on the east end of the garden are perennial flowers. This garden is designed for an active gardener, and the human activity of watering, cutting flowers, and keeping a sharp eye out for bugs is as much a part of the garden as are the flowers.

Behind the annual cut-flower grouping is a lattice arbor with clematis and other vines growing over it.

Following Olmsted and Jekyll in your garden, Wilfred always brings herbs. They represent tradition and the feeling that there is mystery and goodness in the world. In this garden plan, I've put a variety of kitchen and medicinal plants along the central path at the ends of all the garden beds. There they will be easy to gather for use. Friends will stop and talk about them. Skirts and trouser legs will brush against thymes and salvias, liberating their aromas.

At the northwest corner of the plan is a small herbal lawn. Children can roll in the low, tightly matted herbs — chamomile, woolly veronica, lemon thyme. Olmsted would see that an herbal

View

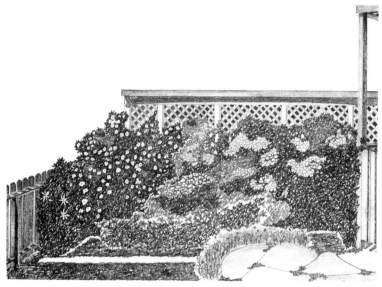

Color

lawn is in line with the genius of the place in Colorado and many other parts of the country.

Herbs like full sun and poor soil. They'll be happy in compacted clay soils if you hold back the water. And water is a resource we need to conserve in many parts of the country. An herbal lawn also requires less fertilizer and less pest control than a conventional sod lawn. In addition, it takes little maintenance, staying naturally so low (about two inches) that mowing is not needed. Herbal lawns do cost more to plant in the first place than grass, but over a period of time that balances out because they cost less to maintain. They can be walked on, but will not take the beating sod will, as on a football field.

In addition to the three herbs I'm using in this herbal lawn, there are several more to choose from. Many varieties of veronica and thyme make low mats, as does creeping yarrow and *Dianthus arvenensis*. If you're not going to be walking on the lawn much, then the list grows much longer, to include violets, dwarf mints, and miniature bulbs. You may also want to sow a few seeds of white clover or other low legume for the fertilizer their nitrogen-fixing roots will provide. The herbal lawn in this garden grows into the flagstone path and creeps up the low rock wall around it.

Onto this garden stage of views, color, and natural order would stride my Chadwickian gardener, bringing the fourth design principle: the drama of balance. "Fill up the garden with luscious vegetables and sweet raspberries, and, outside the fence where there is room, plant delicious fruit trees. The kitchen garden is the most human garden. Here you work and nature responds. Dig the soil, make compost, sow seed, and gather the harvest. Make it beautiful and alive!" he or she would proclaim.

On the garden plan, the areas in the center are double-dug beds for fresh vegetables (and flowers or anything you like) and strawberry beds. Outside the fence are some dwarf fruit trees. Looking

Order

Drama of balance

from the garden *over* the fruit trees, the old farmhouse, the mountains, and nature encompass the garden and all its activity.

Of course, there are hundreds of ways to handle a garden design. No two people will make the same plan for even the same site. The completeness of a design comes from, on the one hand, satisfying the *practical* needs of the site and its gardener(s) *and*, on the other hand, employing your intuitive *imagination* to make it beautiful. Enlist the help of Olmsted, Miss Jekyll, Wilfred, and Chadwick (view, color, order, and the drama of balance) when you walk around your garden site.

To take care of the practical requirements of the site, make a list: you have to get wheelbarrows through gates, fences should be sturdy and keep dogs and winds out, and maintenance and cost must be manageable. As you walk around the site and imagine it becoming a garden, update the list. It will grow. (And sometimes, when you solve three problems with one answer, it will shrink.) Begin to make sketches that satisfy the requirements of time, money, space, and family needs. Erase and try again. You'll get it. All the while, let your imagination quietly contemplate the place — looking for views, and the genius of the place. It all starts from there.

*   *   *

You may not have a whole backyard to garden or the time. Here's a plan for one double-dug bed 4 by 16 feet. The three plans show the bed in spring, summer, and fall. This shows crop rotation, companion planting, and a lot of plants in a very small space.

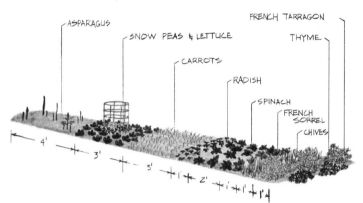

Spring planting

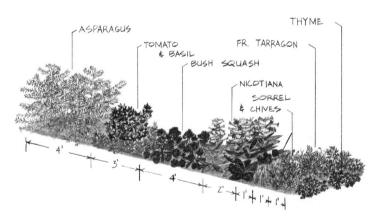

Summer

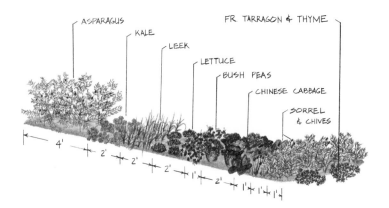

ASPARAGUS
KALE
LEEK
LETTUCE
BUSH PEAS
FR. TARRAGON & THYME
CHINESE CABBAGE
SORREL & CHIVES

4'   2'   2'   2'   1'   2'   1'   1'   1'

Fall

References

Three: Seer and Seen

1. M. Rothschild, "Remarks on Carotenoids in the Evolution of Signals," in *Coevolution of Animals and Plants*, L. Gilbert and P. H. Raven, eds. (Austin: University of Texas Press, 1975), p. 41.

2. *Bulletin of the American Penstemon Society*, December 1978, p. 25.

3. *Bulletin*, p. 28.

Four: From Rice-Making Moon to Temple of the Sun

1. We are indebted to Gardner P. Stickney's account of Ojibwa rice-harvesting practices in the April 1896 issue of *American Anthropologist* (pp. 115–121) for this description.

2. Lester R. Brown and Gail Finsterbusch, *Man and His Environment: Food* (New York: Harper & Row, 1972), p. 23.

3. Quoted in Jack R. Harlan, *Crops and Man* (Madison, WI: American Society of Agronomy, 1975), p. 49.

4. Victor Von Hagen, *Realm of the Inca* (New York: New American Library, 1961), p. 58.

5. Edward Hyams, *Soil and Civilization* (New York: Harper & Row, 1976), p. 223.

6. Hyams, p. 217.

7. Wendell Berry, *The Unsettling of America: Culture and Horticulture* (San Francisco: Sierra Club Books, 1977), p. 178.

Five: The Lineage of the Lawn

1. Laura Wood Roper, *FLO: A Biography* (Baltimore: Johns Hopkins University Press, 1973), p. 71.

2. George E. Chadwick, *The Park and the Town: Public Landscape in the 19th and 20th Centuries* (New York: Praeger, 1966), p. 72.

3. Roper, p. 422.

4. Frederick Law Olmsted, "Instructions to All Engaged in Moving or Planting Trees or Shrubs," Letter of c. June 27, 1860, in *The Papers of Frederick Law Olmsted: Vol. III, Creating Central Park (1857–1861)*, Charles McLaughlin, Editor in Chief (Baltimore: Johns Hopkins University Press, 1983), pp. 254–255.

Six: Aunt Bumps

1. Gertrude Jekyll, *Home and Garden* (Woodbridge, Suffolk, England: Antique Collector's Club, 1981), p. 36.

2. Francis Jekyll, *Gertrude Jekyll: A Memoir* (Northampton, MA: Bookshop Round Table, undated), p. 115.

3. Francis Jekyll, p. 25.

4. Francis Jekyll, p. 48.

5. Francis Jekyll, p. 57.

6. Francis Jekyll, p. 102.

7. Francis Jekyll, p. 82.

8. Gertrude Jekyll, *Wood and Garden* (Salem, NH: Ayer Co., 1983), p. 188.

9. Francis Jekyll, p. 175.

10. Francis Jekyll, p. 195.

11. Francis Jekyll, p. 180.

12. Francis Jekyll, p. 193.

REFERENCES

Seven: St. Wilfred

1. Raef Payne and Wilfred Blunt, *Hortulus* (Pittsburgh: Hunt Botanical Library, 1966), p. 27.
2. Margaret B. Freeman, *Herbs for the Medieval Household* (New York: Metropolitan Museum of Art, 1943), p. 13.
3. Payne and Blunt, p. 37.

Eleven: Year 2: Widening the Cycle

1. Webster Sill, *Plant Protection: An Integrated Interdisciplinary Approach* (Ames, IA: Iowa State University Press, 1982), p. 173.

Reading Guide

For the backyard gardener, the next book I recommend is *Crockett's Victory Garden*, by James Underwood Crockett (Boston: Little, Brown and Company, 1977). This is my favorite gardening book, the one I refer to most frequently. It is a monthly guide to what to do and how to do it for the typical vegetable/flower garden. Mr. Crockett does use chemical fertilizers and pesticides; for those who want to stick with organic materials, do what I do: Substitute. (See the list in appendix C.) Crockett's book is well organized, full of practical detail, and the next best thing to having an old pro at your side.

For the Chadwick method, *How to Grow More Vegetables*, by John Jeavons (Berkeley: Ten Speed Press, 1982) is *the* how-to manual. The illustrations are especially helpful. The bibliography is extensive.

There are many excellent guides to organic methods. *The Self-Sufficient Gardener*, by John Seymour (Garden City, NY: Doubleday, 1980) is well-rounded and authoritative. *Intensive Gardening Round the Year*, by Paul Dorcher, T. Fisher, and K. Kolb (Brattleboro, VT: Stephen Green Press, 1981) has the best chapters I have seen on the history of French intensive market gardening, on how soil, nutrients, and compost work in an intensive bed, and on solar devices. It's an excellent complement to the Jeavons book.

Another book I like very much is *Vegetable Growing Handbook*, by

Walter Splittstoesser (Westport, CT: AVI, 1979). What I like most about this book is that it gives both chemical and organic methods side by side, without prejudice. The reader gets to see both approaches to dealing with many crops, and then make a choice.

Finally, the best source of information is probably your county extension agent. He or she has lots of fact sheets about *local* growing conditions and practices — frost dates, rainfall, varieties that have proven successful in your area — and will undoubtedly know the more active local gardeners, people you want to meet. And local information is the best information — the genius of the place. Remember that the extension service is there for the backyard gardener as well as the farmer. If you want to use organic materials, let your agent know that.

The following is a list of books that pertain to individual chapters of this book. (A listing under one chapter heading may very well also have information relevant to other chapters.)

Part One: Nature's Garden

Virgil, *The Georgics*, Smith Palmer Bovie, trans. (Chicago: University of Chicago Press, 1966).

Helen and Scott Nearing, *Living the Good Life* (New York: Schocken, 1970).

John Davies (Gallup Organization), *1979 National Gardening Association Survey* (Burlington, VT: Gardens for All, 1979).

Elizabeth Yandell, *Henry* (London: Bodley Head, 1974).

One: Through the Garden Gate

Tom Cuthbertson, *Alan Chadwick's Enchanted Garden* (New York: Dutton, 1978).

Videoworks, "Garden Song," 1980. (This 28-minute film, made for PBS, introduces Alan Chadwick and his approach. Another good film is "Garden," directed by Michael Stusser. Both are available from Bullfrog Films, Dept. F, Oley, PA, 19547.)

William Bronson, "The Lesson of a Garden," *Cry California*, Winter 1970-71.

Two: Wild Raspberries

Peter Steinhart, "The Edge Gets Thinner," *Audubon*, Nov. 1983. An in-depth report on soil erosion in the United States today.

Peter Farb, *The Living Soil* (New York: Harper, 1959).

S. R. Eyre, *Vegetation and Soils* (Chicago: Aldine Publishing, 1963).

Henry Gleason and Arthur Cronquist, *The Natural Geography of Plants* (New York: Columbia University Press, 1964).

Sir E. John Russell, *The World of the Soil* (London: Collins, 1967).

Three: Seer and Seen

G. Jon Roush, "On Saving Diversity," *The Nature Conservancy* 32 (1), Jan./Feb. 1982.

John Storer, *The Web of Life* (New York: Signet Key/New American Library, 1953).

L. Gilbert and P. H. Raven, eds., *Coevolution of Animals and Plants* (Austin: University of Texas Press, 1975).

Richard B. Straw, "Adaptive Morphology of the *Penstemon* Flower," *Phytomorphology*, July 1956, pp. 112-119.

Richard B. Straw, "Floral Isolation in Penstemon," *Amer. Naturalist*, Jan./Feb. 1956, pp. 17-53.

Ann Zwinger, *Beyond the Aspen Grove* (New York: Harper, 1981).

Alfred S. Romer, *The Procession of Life* (New York: Doubleday, 1972).

Loren Eiseley, *The Immense Journey* (New York: Random House, 1957).

Anthony Huxley, *Plant and Planet* (New York: Penguin, 1978).

P. J. Darlington, *Evolution for Naturalists* (New York: Wiley, 1980).

B. J. D. Meeuse, *The Story of Pollination* (New York: Ronald Press, 1961).

Verne Grant, *The Hummingbird and Its Flowers* (New York: Columbia University Press, 1968).

Four: From Rice-Making Moon to Temple of the Sun

Jack Harlan, *Crops and Man* (Madison, WI: American Society of Agronomy, 1975).

Edgar Anderson, *Plants, Man, and Life* (Berkeley: University of California Press, 1969).

Lester R. Brown and Gail Finsterbusch, *Man and His Environment: Food* (New York: Harper & Row, 1972).

Franz Schwanitz, *The Origin of Cultivated Plants* (Cambridge, MA: Harvard University Press, 1966).

Edward Hyams, *Soil and Civilization* (New York: Harper & Row, 1976).

Tom Dale and Vernon Carter, *Topsoil and Civilization* (Norman, OK: University of Oklahoma Press, 1955).

Wendell Berry, *The Unsettling of America: Culture and Agriculture* (San Francisco: Sierra Club Books, 1977).

Victor Von Hagen, *Realm of the Incas* (New York: New American Library, 1961).

Part Two: Garden Masters

Kenneth Clark, *What Is a Masterpiece?* (London: Thames and Hudson, 1979).

Edward Hyams, *A History of Gardens and Gardening* (New York: Praeger, 1971).

Five: The Lineage of the Lawn

David Jarrett, *The English Landscape Garden* (New York: Rizzoli, 1978).

John Dixon Hunt and Peter Willis, eds., *The Genius of the Place: The English Landscape Garden 1620–1820* (New York: Harper & Row, 1975).

Laura Wood Roper, *FLO: A Biography* (Baltimore: Johns Hopkins University Press, 1973).

Elizabeth Stevenson, *Park Maker: A Life of Frederick Law Olmsted* (New York: Macmillan, 1977).

George F. Chadwick, *The Park and the Town: Public Landscape in the 19th and 20th Centuries* (New York: Praeger, 1966).

Elizabeth Barlow, ed., *The Central Park Book* (New York: Central Park Task Force, 1977).

R. Gerard Koskovich, "Frederick Law Olmsted and the Original Landscape Plans for Stanford University," unpublished manuscript, Stanford University archives, 1982.

Six: Aunt Bumps

Gertrude Jekyll, *Wood and Garden* (Woodbridge, Suffolk, England: Antique Collector's Club, 1981).

Gertrude Jekyll, *Home and Garden* (Woodbridge, Suffolk, England: Antique Collector's Club, 1981).

Gertrude Jekyll, *Colour Schemes for the Flower Garden* (Woodbridge, Suffolk, England: Antique Collector's Club, 1983).

Francis Jekyll, *Gertrude Jekyll: A Memoir* (Northampton, MA: Bookshop Round Table, undated).

Roy Genders, *The Cottage Garden* (London: Pelham, 1983).

Jane Brown, *Gardens of a Golden Afternoon* (New York: Van Nostrand, 1982).

Gertrude Jekyll, *Old English Household Life* (London: Betsford, 1975).

Betty Massingham, *Miss Jekyll: Portrait of a Great Gardener* (London: Country Life, 1966).

Anne Scott-James, *Sissinghurst, The Making of a Garden* (London: Michael Joseph, 1975).

Arno and Irene Nehrling, *Gardening for Flower Arrangement* (New York: Dover, 1969).

Seven: St. Wilfred

Walafried of Strabo, *The Hortulus*, Raef Payne, trans. (Pittsburgh: Hunt Botanical Library, 1966).

Margaret B. Freeman, *Herbs for the Medieval Household* (New York: Metropolitan Museum of Art, 1943).

Eleanor Sinclair Rohde, *The Old English Herbals* (London: Longman, Green and Co., 1922).

Maude Grieve, *A Modern Herbal* (New York: Dover, 1982).

Eight: This Too Could Be Yours

Alan Chadwick Society, *The Chadwick Society Newsletter*, Green Gulch Farm, Star Route 1, Sausalito, CA 94965.

Wolf D. Storl, *Culture and Horticulture* (Wyoming, RI: Biodynamic Literature, 1979).

Part Three: The Practice of Gardening

Hugh Johnson, *The Principles of Gardening* (New York: Simon and Schuster, 1979). This is the best introduction to the *world* of gardening, from plant roots to flower gardens to garden history. Succinct, accurate, inspiring.

Catherine Osgood Foster, *The Organic Gardener* (New York: Random House, 1972).

Alan Titchmarsh, *Gardening Techniques* (New York: Simon and Schuster, 1981).

Nine: Thinking Like a Seed

J. K. A. Bleasdale, *Plant Physiology in Relation to Horticulture* (London: Macmillan, 1979).

Look for a good guide to your local flora and natural history. As you learn the herbs, wildflowers, and native edible plants of your area, you learn about your growing conditions and the plant groups that like to grow there. For Colorado, I like:

251

Ruth Ashton Nelson, *Handbook of Rocky Mountain Plants* (Estes Park, CO: Skyland, 1979).

H. D. Harrington, *Edible Native Plants of the Rocky Mountains* (Albuquerque: University of New Mexico Press, 1967).

Cornelia Fleischer Mutel and John C. Emerick, *From Grassland to Glacier: The Natural History of Colorado* (Boulder, CO: Johnson Books, 1984).

William A. Weber, *Rocky Mountain Flora* (Boulder, CO: Colorado Associated University Press, 1976).

Ten: The Basic Cycle: Year 1

James Underwood Crockett, *Crockett's Victory Garden* (Boston: Little, Brown, 1977). Best monthly guide.

John Jeavons, *How to Grow More Vegetables* (Berkeley: Ten Speed Press, 1982). Best how-to manual for the Chadwick method.

Chris Catton and James Gray, *The Incredible Heap* (New York: St. Martin's Press, 1983). Clear and simple on how to make and use compost.

Marny Smith, *Gardening with Conscience* (New York: Seabury/Vineyard, 1981). Very good on intensive backyard gardening.

Eleven: Year 2: The Widening Cycle

Pests

John and Helen Philbrick, *The Bug Book* (Wilkinsonville, MA: Philbrick, 1963).

Helen Philbrick and Richard Gregg, *Companion Plants and How to Use Them* (Old Greenwich, CT: Devin-Adair, 1966).

Webster B. Sill, *Plant Protection: An Integrated Interdisciplinary Approach* (Ames, IA: Iowa State University Press, 1982).

Robert van den Bosch and Mary Louise Flint, *Introduction to Integrated Pest Management* (New York: Plenum Press, 1981).

John H. Perkins, *Insects, Experts, and the Insecticide Crisis* (New York: Plenum Press, 1982).

•

Edwin Way Teale, *Strange Lives of Familiar Insects* (New York: Dodd, Mead, 1962).

Soil Improvement

H. H. Koepf, *Compost* (Wyoming, RI: Biodynamic Farming and Gardening Association, Number 77, undated).

G. W. Cooke, *Control of Soil Fertility* (New York: Hafner, 1967).

Otto Schmid and Ruedi Klay, *Green Manuring: Principles and Practice*, William Brinton, trans. (Temple, ME: Woods End Agricultural Institute, 1981).

Richard Jackson and Frank Raw, *Life in the Soil* (New York: Edward Arnold, 1966).

Henry Hopp, *About Earthworms* (Charlotte, VT: Garden Way, 1973).

Vegetable Gardening

Tony Biggs, *Vegetables* (New York: Simon and Schuster/RHS, 1980). Clear, concise, well-illustrated.

Albert C. Burrage, *Burrage on Vegetables*, revised by Susan and Timothy Hollander (Boston: Houghton Mifflin, 1975).

Helen M. Fox, *Gardening for Good Eating* (New York: Collier/Macmillan, 1974). Excellent. Emphasis on flavor.

Fruit Culture

Harry Baker, *Fruit* (New York: Simon and Schuster/RHS, 1980). Another well-illustrated how-to book in the Simon and Schuster/RHS series.

S. R. Williams, *Compost Fruit Growing* (London: Foulsham, 1961).

H. P. Hedrick, *Fruits for the Home Garden* (New York: Dover, 1973).

Pomona, Journal of the North American Fruit Explorers, c/o Mary Kurle, 10 S. 055 Madison St., Hinsdale, IL 60521. A friendly little journal for the backyard grower and fruit enthusiast.

Twelve: Real Wealth

Henry David Thoreau, *Walden* (Garden City, NY: Doubleday, 1981).

"Walden" and "Farm Paper" in E. B. White, *One Man's Meat* (New York: Harper, 1983), and "A Slight Sound at Evening," in E. B. White, *The Points of My Compass* (New York: Harper, 1962).

Gene Logsdon, *Homesteading* (Emmaus, PA: Rodale, 1973).

John and Sally Seymour, *Farming for Self-Sufficiency* (New York: Schocken, 1976).

John Jeavons, J. Mogador Griffin, and Robin Leler, *Backyard Homestead Mini-Farm* (Berkeley: Ten Speed Press, 1983).

Peter Henderson, *Gardening for Profit* (New York: Orange Judd, 1882).

R. Neil Sampson, *Farmland or Wasteland* (Emmaus, PA: Rodale, 1981).

Ehrenfried Pfeiffer, *The Earth's Face and Human Destiny* (Emmaus, PA: Rodale, 1947).

B. Stonehouse, ed., *Biological Husbandry: A scientific approach to organic farming* (London: Butterworth, 1981).

D. F. Bezdicek, ed., *Organic Farming: Current Technology and Its Role in Sustainable Agriculture* (Madison, WI: American Society of Agronomy, 1984).